Simple as That

A SIMPLE GUIDE TO LIVING IN ABUNDANCE

TERRY MEER

Deep Roots Publishing

SEBASTIAN, FLORIDA

Deep Roots Publishing

11155 Roseland Road

Sebastian, Florida 32958

Ordering Information:

Quantity sales. Special discounts are available on quantity purchases by corporations, associations, and others. For details, contact the "Special Sales Department" at the address above.

Simple as That/ Terry Meer. —1st ed.

ISBN 978-1-7366411-0-1

Contents

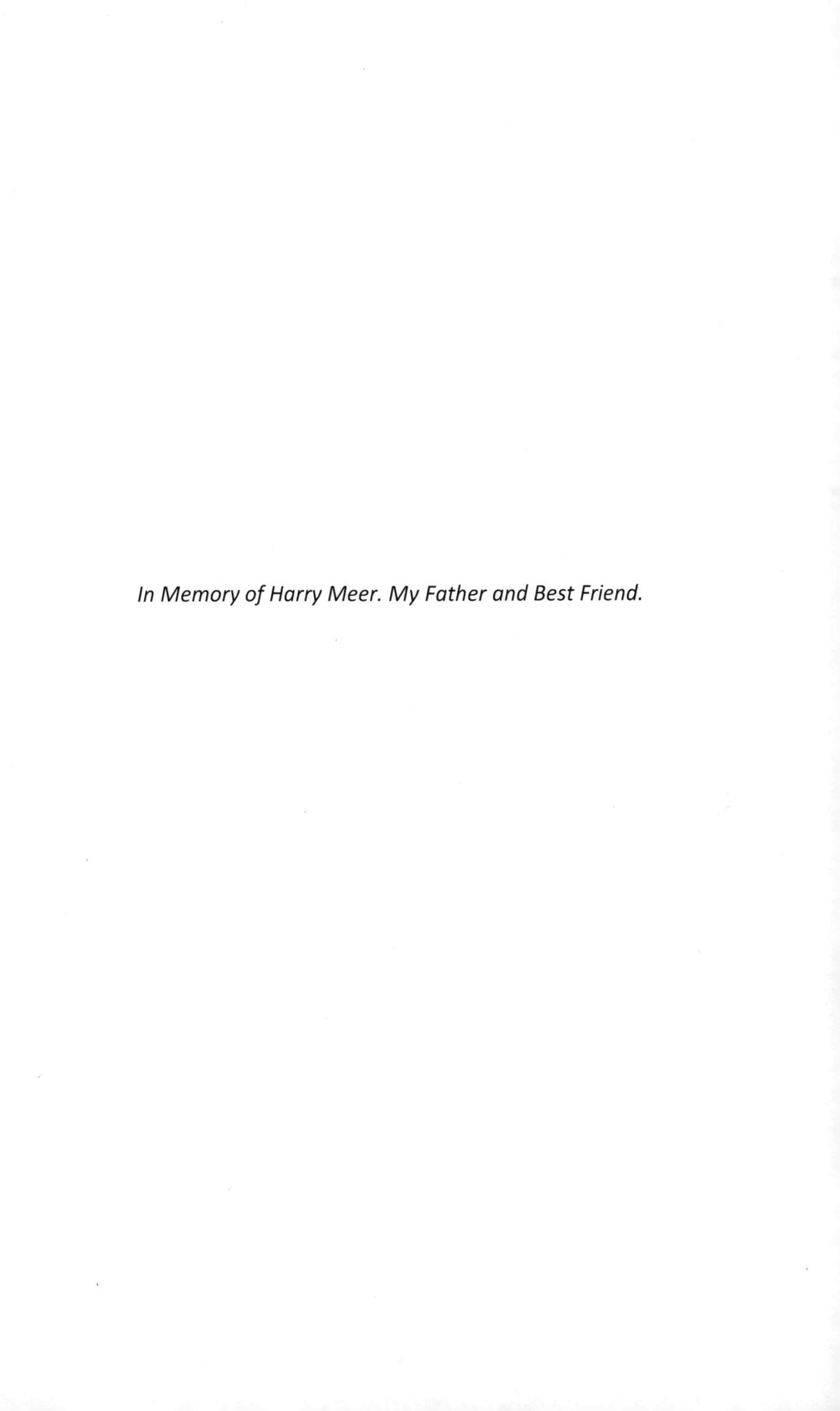

In Memory of Harry Meer. My Father and Best Friend.

There is no other path for us than that of cooperative productivity and community responsibility. Take that path, and it will change your life in ways you cannot yet imagine.

—Bill Mollison - Father of Permaculture

Acknowledgments

Thank you to everyone who made this book possible. I never could have done it without you all. I especially would like to thank Amy, Kashi Lynn, and Matagiri for the hours of selfless co-creation and editing that made it happen. I also want to thank Jaya, Dylan, and Drew for adding their brilliant artistic talents to the project.

There are many others through my life that I have shared my journeys with. Thank you from the depths of my heart.

CHAPTER 1

Spokes in the Wheel

"Look deep into nature and then you will understand everything better."

- Albert Einstein

DO YOU KNOW SOMEONE who wakes up every morning feeling disconnected? Do you know someone who wishes they were living their passion in life?

This book is a collection of the most valuable lessons and tools I have learned in my journey on planet Earth. I am going to demonstrate how I use these tools to build a bridge between a healthy ecosystem and a thriving landscape within my own heart. I will introduce the concept of a "regenerative lifestyle" to help us all create abundance and prosperity by putting our dreams into action while providing service to humanity.

Over the last several decades, we have seen exponential population growth, significant increases in fossil fuel extractions, and a steady decline in the health of our oceans and coral reefs. All this environmental degradation has been met with a steady increase in personal stress, disease, and anxiety in the human population. It has become apparent to me that humans have strayed from the path of health and happiness and need to return to a way of life that is more in balance with nature.

Everyone reading this book has a different vision of a perfect life, yet the tools and techniques to arrive at this goal can be very similar. As we complete this bridge between our perfect life and a healthy ecosystem, we will create true abundance by embracing a lifestyle that nurtures both our highest selves and our precious planet so future generations can enjoy the abundance.

Let me begin by introducing myself. At the time of writing this book, I am living aboard my 29-foot off-grid floating tiny house. I am exploring my childhood dream of living aboard a blue water sailboat named "Resilience" while teaching permaculture and writing books. I love my job and I get to travel around the world to places I have always wanted to go and teach the most amazing people how to create abundance. I have loving friends and would not change any part of my life. So, how did I get here?

I started this life at sea, aboard a beautiful 35-foot wooden sailboat named the "Ariva" which was made in the islands of Hawaii. My parents could best be described as hippie pirates who were not interested in joining society in any way. As her due date grew closer, my mother, being a true nature spirit, decided that I would be born on board and in nature. She went into labor in Dinner Key, a small lagoon in South Miami. I imagine it was quite a bit more challenging than she originally imagined because the family took an adventurous bus ride to Jackson Memorial Hospital at 2 a.m. where I physically entered this world.

After my short stay in the hospital, I moved back onto what would be my home for the next 5 years: a small hammock hung from the forward main berth of the boat. We sailed many miles in those first five years, exploring remote islands in the Bahamas and finding new ports for fresh food and supplies. Swimming, fishing, and collecting water were some of the typical daily activities our seaward family would enjoy. This was my life, my playground, and my school.

Boat life turned out to be too much for my parents' relationship. When I was two years old, my mother stepped off the boat and I never saw her again. It took me many years to realize the pain this abandonment planted in me. I buried it deep inside and it wasn't until my late 30s that I began to address it.

My father remarried, this time to a beautiful woman named Betty. She had 3 children from a previous marriage, so my father sold the "Ariva" when I was six years old and bought a 50-foot pontoon houseboat named the "Hootch". The "Hootch" was quite an upgrade with a sundeck, living room, and bunk beds for our growing family, which now included five children, two adults, and our beloved 85-pound Golden Retriever named Homer.

Life was simple on the Hootch. Our hot-water tank was a 50-gallon barrel painted black. Right next to it was our cold-water tank was a 50-gallon barrel painted white. If I wanted to take a hot shower, I waited until after 11:00 a.m. on a sunny day. This was my first lesson in non-attachment. I realized early that the idea of being in control of everything was an illusion. I had to surrender to the cycles of nature. I discovered I had adopted a rhythm based on these natural patterns. I also learned conservation early in life while living on the boat. In the shower, I turned the water off while soaping up my body and never took longer than 5 minutes to get clean. I never thought of this as unusual or difficult. I just remember being so grateful when the tanks were full and the water was hot.

I learned gratitude very early. I like to think the unique beginnings of my life freed me from the typical mindset of mainstream consumerism in

America. I just understood that the amount of water in the sink had a limit. We did not have the luxury of putting trash outside to make it go away. There was no "away". We did not have a car. Everything was in balance with the ecosystem around us. Everything was connected and simple.

This life of conservation was rewarded with beautiful sunsets, an abundance of time with family, and a deep connection with nature that few people get to experience.

When I was 10 years old, I learned that my grandmother did not appreciate the hippie pirate life we were living so she told my father that we children needed a stable environment and needed to go to a real school. My father gave us the choice to continue on the boat or go live with my grandmother. I wanted to experience the regular life everyone said was so amazing and made my choice to live with her. I often wonder what my life would be now if I had chosen to stay on the boat.

My grandmother was a retired flight attendant and lived in Melbourne, Florida. She retired there because it was a quiet, beautiful little beach town. She was an active part of a local retirement club and her community loved her. The move for me however, was a complete transformation from my previous life aboard the sailboat.

I remember this as one of the most awkward times in my life. I went to a regular school with regular kids. There was an endless supply of hot water but I had to wear shoes. I realized the conversations I had changed from what the clouds resembled to what was on TV last night. I noticed my relationships became less deep and observed that people didn't really connect with each other. I had a lot of adjusting to do to fit into this new world.

After moving off the boat and into a normal life, the biggest shift I noticed was a collective agreement that humanity lived in a world of scarcity. It seemed there was never enough time, money, or whatever else you needed. I realized that this underlying scarcity created a constant fear which motivated people to do things they did not want to do, such as working a job they did not like in order to make money. I realized people believed they were force to do these things or they wouldn't have enough to survive. I instantly knew that I did not resonate with this new paradigm.

After getting my high school diploma in 1992, I decided it was time to see the world. I bought a 1973 orange Volkswagen bus and started driving. I went to many festivals and concerts and sold lots of grilled cheese sandwiches in Grateful Dead parking lots. The community I saw in the festival scene captivated me. People were taking care of each other and having fun together. I was like a moth to a flame and was brought to the next chapter of my personal development when I found the Rainbow Family of Living Light. This is a group of travelers and explorers started by a few hippies back in the '70s. They travel to different national forests as one big family seeking community and spiritual healing.

When I was at my first gathering in Ocala, Florida, a beaded, bearded stranger looked at me and said, "Welcome home!" In that moment I knew I had found something special—a sense of community and belonging. I continued traveling, looking for more communities similar to the one I had found. I explored Costa Rica, Mexico, and anywhere I could find people living together in community.

In 1997, I decided to go back to Melbourne, Florida, start college, and take care of my grandmother. In 2001, I graduated from the University of Central Florida from the College of Health and Public Affairs and spent the next 10 years serving children with Autism as a Behavior Analyst. This was the beginning of my corporate years.

Eventually, I was promoted to Clinical Quality Management for Deveraux where I sat in my office, perched upon the 27th floor, and read clinical files all day long. I was making more money than I could spend, successfully climbing the corporate ladder, and I was completely and totally unfulfilled and isolated. This materialistic corporate life was not what my spirit wanted to do all day and I just knew that there had to be something more exciting. This is where I began my work of aligning myself with my true nature and passion.

My Father taught me that there are three rules in life:

- **Number 1** Nothing, at anytime, anywhere, matters.
- **Number 2** Keeping #1 in mind, find something that does matter.
- **Number 3** Still keeping #1 in mind, hold onto it with everything you have got.

I was thinking about these rules as I was riding the elevator one morning to my 27th-floor corporate job, when an exhausted co-worker sighed and said to me, “It’s almost Friday.” Every muscle in my body tensed. It was only Monday. I realized I couldn’t stay in this empty world any longer, wishing my days away, living for the weekend, feeling no passion for my work. It was at that moment that I realized I wanted to explore sacred ecology before I even knew what sacred ecology was. I walked out of the elevator and right into the HR department to figure out the next steps of my new life.

As I was leaving my corporate job, I started searching for new systems of environmental connection. I knew there had to be a holistic way of connecting our personal passions with the needs of our community and our ecosystem. This brought me to the wonderful world of Permaculture.

Permaculture is a design science that imitates natural systems in order to create abundance. A man named Bill Mollison started it in Australia with his friend David Holmgren. They expressed that we can design and use food, energy, and water in a way that they can provide what is needed for other productive systems around us. This creates more abundant and healthy systems that are easier to maintain. Permaculture combines community, food, health, and ecology to create a whole system of abundance. I jumped in with both feet and started taking every class I could find on the subject.

I studied many aspects of ecology, beginning with my earliest research reading the works of American biologist Eugene Odom including, “Fundamentals of Ecology,” and, “Ecological Vignettes.“ It was through this study that I began looking at ecology as a relationship within nature rather than a way of measuring available resources for extraction. I soon began to study “closed-loop” systems, which do not require external input or resources to keep them running. They thrive on the yields of other elements within the larger system. Imagine a natural forest system: nobody carries mulch or fertilizer to feed the forest. The detritus, or dead plant material from the trees, fall on the forest floor, creating ground cover and habitat for microorganisms in the soil. These microorganisms create nutrients for the plants. The plants produce food for animals. The animals produce fertilizer and food for larger animals. The system thrives and regenerates.

Permaculture is a way of thinking which offers us a nature-based framework to utilize our "waste" and reconnect it into our ecosystem. Nutrients are cycled and there is homeostasis or balance. Humans, being the amazingly intelligent and resourceful creatures we are, have created ways to use more than just one day's worth of solar energy every day. We started digging up fossil fuels, capping natural gas lines, and creating many other destructive methods of energy production. Everything on this planet gets energy from the sun. As one day of sunlight hits our planet the plants create one day's worth of energy in the form of organic material and growth. Currently, we are using many years' worth of energy created by the sun to support one day's worth of human activity. This is not only unsustainable, but also irresponsible to future generations of humans and all other species on the planet.

In our consumerist society, we have been trained to put our focus on money, security, and how shiny our cars are. I have decided to write this book to share my belief that we have been sold a broken system. I see the entire design as flawed. The more time spent chasing material wealth and social stature, the more we are not living our dreams and the more we lower the vibration of everyone and everything around us. We slowly turn into unhappy, unmotivated, and unfulfilled people with really shiny cars. I see people today working jobs they do not want and sacrificing time with family and the fulfillment of their dreams because they're afraid of not having enough. This fear-based way of thinking limits our true potential in this beautiful life. Once we start living in a world built on responsibility to our entire ecosystem, trust, love, and compassion, we can realize that abundance is all around us.

The only thing we need to do to change society is to convince society that we can change. I saw a four-year-old child's face light up in amazement as she dug up a fresh carrot for the first time and I have seen hope in a 20-year-old inspired by learning how to make bio char to use in his garden to grow his own food. More and more I get to see people dedicated to the idea of living in balance with our ecosystem, finding a bridge between a healthy ecosystem and living an abundant human life filled with passion. I believe there is hope, and that this hope is easiest to see in the individuals consciously choosing to live simpler lives and making positive environmental changes.

We could all drive less, turn off and unplug appliances, gain awareness of where our food and energy come from, and have compassion for those who do not have the luxuries we take for granted. I have lived on boats, in tiny houses, and tents which provided me with a simple framework of living without many of the modern convinces of modern life. Growing up on the boat helped me appreciate our fragile connection to the earth. This created a mindset that I've carried with me my entire life: all resources are precious and we are all connected just as all human are precious and stronger when connected. I believe many humans will benefit from this way of thinking and I hope that I am successful in expressing my beliefs to you in these pages. There has never been a better time to pay attention to the earth and reconnect with her. Terrance McKenna once said, “Nature is not mute; it is man who is deaf.”

I believe it is time to remember how to hear her once again.

How to Use this Book

Simple as That is designed to help refocus the way we live our lives. It is divided into 12 chapters that you can imagine as 12 spokes of a wheel. The wheel represents an abundant and fulfilling life. Each spoke is equally important to the strength of the entire wheel. All of the chapters are connected and you may start see connecting or overlapping concepts as you read. Try to visualize how each chapter relates to the others.

Take your time with each chapter. I recommend reading one chapter at a time and spending time doing the activities at the end of the chapter before starting the next chapter. These ten activities are tools designed as a springboard to help you realize your passion and start living the life you have always dreamed. The activities build on each other and I recommend doing them in order. The more you do the activities; you may be amazed at how quickly opportunities present themselves as you design your life to be more integrated with itself and begin to live more connected with the world around you.

I strongly believe that if you follow the simple guidelines in this book, you can build a strong relationship and connection with nature and humanity resulting in more abundance in your life. As you tend your inner garden with intent, you will find the physical world shifts to reflect that beautiful garden.

I wrote this book as a simple guide to illuminate the patterns I have discovered in my life that I feel have raised my conscious vibration to one of happiness, joy, compassion, and abundance.

It is very important to keep an open mind and be willing to look at yourself through new eyes every day. Let's get started.

CHAPTER 2

Love and Gratitude

"When you are grateful, fear disappears and abundance appears."

- Anthony Robbins

LOVE AND GRATITUDE serves as the foundation for all the chapters of this book. I have found there are few things in the universe that are more important than love and gratitude. I believe that the true nectar of this life is when we find the motivation and the courage to put our love into action. In this book, we will call this "finding your passion in life."

Have you ever started doing something, perhaps drawing or playing music, and time just disappeared? Perhaps something you thought would take only a few minutes turns into timelessness. This same phenomenon happens to yogis during meditation and cyclists during bike rides. When we enter this state of consciousness, we become hypersensitive to the natural world around us. This is our natural state, our true state of existence.

My best teacher in this life is nature herself; the forest is my favorite classroom. I find myself just sitting and observing all the intricate relationships that exist. Sitting in nature, I get the opportunity to learn patience, joy, acceptance, and triumph. I cannot pretend to understand even one percent of everything that is going on, but I enjoy just being present in the symphony.

I spent over 5 years as the Director of a sustainability program on an 80-acre intentional community where I taught hundreds of people yearly to live in balance with the earth. It was a position where I introduced people to living off-grid in nature for three-week periods. I appreciated seeing people that have never been in nature find a new love for the primitive world. I like saying my job was to take people into nature and try to get them to stay longer. I have observed the reintroduction process hundreds of different times and there are usually quite a few similarities.

The first step I typically saw was amazement from the beauty nature has to offer. People naturally crave that connection with the Earth and start to release the tension learned from the past and expand into the present. There is a type of love here that is unlike any other—different from that of a parent or a child. This type of love is innate and built into our very being. The love of nature is engrained within our true self.

For billions of years, nature has been learning and growing. She has patiently evolved into her current form of perfection. Each system is seamlessly integrated into the next, each regenerating and recharging itself. As humans we spend our time trying to dissect each of these systems and labeling them as separate parts. When you think of the cells in our body as something separate from our bodies it becomes easier to think of each of us as separate from the earth and the earth separate from the universe and so on. This is the foundation of a method of thought based on separation and disconnection needed to justify the destruction of our environment in exchange for profit and convenience.

Nature's gentle perfection is easy to see when I observe humans attempt to control and improve her design. We create wasteful linear systems with no thought of how those systems affect others. By comparison, nature heals as she grows and produces abundance. Nature holds all of us like a mother holds her child. She keeps us safe and creates the perfect environment for us to grow. In this perfect container we are free to explore our potential to share with the world. Because of the priceless gifts nature has bestowed to humanity, we have been able to evolve into the most intelligent apex species currently on the planet. It fills my heart with gratitude when I think of how precious these gifts really are.

I can still remember the day when I realized the life-changing truth that we are nature! Our very essence is meant to flow within this perfect system. I used to think humans somehow became more powerful than nature, as if that were possible, as though we were allowed to make a whole new set of rules because of our superior intellect. Now I realize we just made up our own labels and nature's rules have not been changed at all. Nature does not play by our rules. Nature does not know compassion or hate. These are human words that explain human emotions and beliefs. Nature is so much older than that. I now believe that our purpose here is to offer our human compassion to nature and help create a more peaceful oasis.

When I feel overwhelmed or stressed by the current state of our world, I try to put everything into a simpler perspective. I like to look at life as a perfect painting. Everything that has ever been is painted on this amazing collage of eternity. I see nature as the canvas on which it's all painted. Every dinosaur and every tree are painted here. The entire human experience has also been sketched. Every religion, every war, every child's laughter has been skillfully rendered and represented on this infinite canvas. When I view life as this painting, I realize just what small part humanity occupies. We are so new and so small that the entirety of the human legacy would only take up a tiny corner. With all our debates over money, technology, culture, and the illusion of intelligence, we only cover a minuscule portion on the canvas. Additionally, we are each a part of this amazing painting and we all have the gift to paint it in any way we choose. We choose what to paint, we choose the colors to use, and the colors we choose will produce our moods and the opportunities we find in life. With this awareness and perspective, it is hard to imagine why we would waste this gift painting stress, anxiety, resentment, greed, and destruction.

We are seeing a significant increase in depression and mental illness in the general population today. I believe there is a direct correlation between our decreasing happiness as a culture and the growing disconnection we experience with nature. In order to be rooted in love, we must all care for the ecosystem as we would for our own bodies. We drive cars, burn fossil fuels, and engage in ridiculous levels of consumption and waste with the full awareness that this lifestyle is destroying the very planet on which we live. I do not see how it is possible to experience true inner peace knowing that our way of life is destroying the possibility of a healthy existence for the future generations of all species on earth.

To have come to realize I have the power to be part of the natural cycle of nutrients to help align/steer/guide the natural cycle of nutrients in the least wasteful, most productive way. This is one of the most empowering feelings I have experienced. This is clearly demonstrated in the indescribable feeling I get when I compost. I pretend I am a sorcerer as I magically turn a banana peel into fertile soil that I can then use in another ancient spell to grow a tiny seed into a full-grown radish in only 30 days! This is nature's true alchemy; more precious than gold, and the connection fills me with joy, happiness, and love. I am part of the river that has been flowing for millions of years; I am connected to life.

Once, I was asked how I find the time for all of the additional permaculture projects in my life. My simple answer was I don't have to find time to add any of these things into my life; these things are my life. I get far more satisfaction composting and growing food than I ever could by watching television or sitting on the couch. We have become a society of observers, watching the destruction of our home. I see so many people working jobs they do not like and then wasting time after work with mind-numbing activities only to wonder why they do not feel fulfilled. This felt like running on a hamster wheel to me and I had to find a better way.

Returning in 2017 from a three-month sabbatical in New Zealand, I began talking to a woman next to me on the plane. I told her it was time for me to return to my job and my travels were over for the summer. She replied in a defeated sigh, "Back to real life." This struck me as strange in that moment, but I did not realize why until later. You see, the statement she made implied that my real life was something I needed to get away from. That was not the truth. I love my job. I love to grow food. I love to compost food. I love to be an active part in sharing nature with open-minded people. I soon realized that when we live our true passions in this life, we never need a vacation again. We don't say things like, "I need to get away." Instead, we wake up every day into a continuing adventure of living our lives.

You will find endless new possibilities materialize when you start each day with love and gratitude. It is easy to get frustrated in this world of constant challenges. It is a practice to approach those challenges with patience and awareness. There are many tools such as breath work, meditation, and yoga to help focus the mind. I invite you to try this simple practice that has changed my life:

As you wake up in the morning, spend just five minutes listing some of the things for which you are grateful. I was very resistant to this practice at first, but eventually, I started saying just one thing I was grateful for. I would lie in bed and say something like, "I am grateful for my friends," or, "I am grateful for this new day." One thing slowly turned into two things, two things turned into four things, and now it is not uncommon for me to just lie in bed for an hour giggling about how many things fill my life with gratitude.

When we take the time to create this gratitude bubble around us, it is hard for all the little things that show up in our days to get us down. To be stuck in the mud is something completely different than being stuck in the mud with gratitude. It becomes exciting to jump out of bed and start the new, beautiful day filled with love and gratitude.

As you are in your day and realize you are getting frustrated, thank yourself for observing this state of mind. Stop and take five deep breaths.

Then remember your morning gratitude list. You may find this makes even the most frustrating situation just melt away.

I have learned to see only the best in the people around me. I have been in circles where people speak negatively about others or talk about the horrible things in the world. This kind of talk will never take us to our highest potential; it can only bring the group vibration level down. I discovered that this is a cycle we create that causes us to close our hearts to others. This closing creates awkward situations that manifest in the world as difficult situations.

I learned to see others in their best light, and see them as more than the worst decisions they have made. This change in perception builds a solid foundation of love and respect between us. These stronger relationships are the seeds for so many of life's most meaningful opportunities and experiences.

As I fill my life with inspirational and uplifting relationships, it is much easier to live an inspired, inspirational, and uplifting life. We are creating our lives every day. I learned that I have control of my relationships and how I interact with others. I do not have control over everything that happens to me, but I do have control over how I consciously respond (rather than react) to them. The more I choose to respond with love, forgiveness, and compassion, the more I have seen those situations transform into some of my most precious memories.

Every moment, you have the opportunity to choose a life filled with love and gratitude. You really do have the power to shape your life.

Imagine you are standing facing a wall. You are standing so close to the wall that all you can see is what is directly in front of your face. This is how I explain the majority of our society living today, only thinking about what they need to do and only focused on what is wrong in life. Now imagine backing up a few steps. You can see the window a few feet away. Now back up a few more steps. You can now see the roof and the building next door. Each time you back up, you add more into your field of vision. Each thing in the frame is another opportunity and a new relationship. With this expanded awareness, abundance starts to appear around us in the form of friends, love, and joy.

"How did you take those first steps back to start moving forward?" you ask. I simply let go of the illusion that I was in complete control and that I knew exactly how things should unfold. I stopped blocking all the good things that I didn't know existed from showing up in my life by not clutching onto limited, preconceived visions of the future. I accepted that there are far more wonderful and amazing things in this world than the ones I accepted as reality. I started saying, "yes" to all the new opportunities that appeared as I continued to "back up" from the wall. Now I am not afraid to approach each new day with the fresh eyes of a child and an open mind. I say, "Yes," to life. I try to enjoy the sacred connection I have with everything in this universe. When I meet someone new, I look at the situation as an opportunity to meet a new part of myself. I see a chance to love in a new way and open my heart just a little more. I have learned to be grateful and look for ways to help people without looking for anything in return.

I studied some work of Charles Eisenstein called Sacred Economics, wherein he details the effects of investing in groups of people rather than for personal profit. I have seen the benefits that service-based communities provide and have seen these communities filled with love, laughter, and happiness, compared to the greed and competition I have become familiar with in large cities. When we see the connection we have with each other and create a foundation of love and gratitude, we have the opportunity to recognize that we are just one life with many faces. We are interconnected. We are nature. We can live abundant lives with open hearts that will not allow the mind to separate us.

As you begin to live a life built on a foundation of love and gratitude and start seeing the best in others, you may discover an unexpected treasure: self-love. This lesson seems to have taken the longest for me in my journey. Growing up, I always found my happiness by making others happy. I would latch on to their happiness, unable to create my own. This became clear to me later in life. If I were making breakfast for someone I love, I would make the best Belgian waffles or crepes with fresh fruit and flowers. If I were making breakfast for myself, I might make a very plain bowl of cereal or, more likely, skip breakfast altogether. I realized I never put energy into spoiling myself like I did others. Making a special breakfast for someone else took lots of time and energy but I enjoyed making them happy and I wanted to impress them. I didn't think I was worth taking the time for myself. That realization was the beginning of my journey into self-love.

I spent a lot of time in reflection on why I did not think I was good enough. Out of the hundreds of people that have gone through my programs, the most common personal challenges people have shared with me is this lack of self-love and worthiness.

I like to imagine that we are born into this world perfect. As we get older, we painfully add reasons why we are not. Perhaps it is our appearance or a physical limitation, but these are just stories that we tell ourselves to try and convince us that we are not good enough or that we should not even try. We must rewrite the story and return to that beautiful vision of ourselves.

We are manifestations of pure light with perfect molecules running through our whole bodies, creating powerful vessels that will achieve amazing things. I have accepted this as truth and now make time to spoil myself. I believe that this is one of the best decisions I have made in this life.

There is a state of indestructible and unconditional love that exists. I have seen this loving state appear in new parents after childbirth. There seems there is nothing that the new child could do to make this love diminish. I believe our natural state is love. As we get older, we begin to add reasons why we cannot love people. Perhaps we choose to separate people because they are of a different religion, race, or sexual preference but these are just illusions that take us away from our natural state of unconditional love. I have made myself a promise to live in a world of compassion for all. I will not settle for anything less or be led off of this path of kindness. I will walk away from all of the things that do not lift the global vibration to place that offers supports to everyone with love in their hearts so that we can all share this world of love and abundance.

I keep a quote in my heart that guides me in this practice by the esteemed Dr. Martin Luther King who said: "No one is free until we all are free." This quote is equally true whether the subject is racial equality, LGBTQ rights, or any other segment of social justice. If we remember that we are all connected on the foundation of love and kindness the divisionary details can fade into the background as we allow a more tolerant and compassionate unification to come into focus.

Activity 1:
What is your passion?

Finding your passion in life may be one of the most important things you can do. There has never been a better time than right now to identify this passion and add it into your daily routine.

- •Take time to sit in a quiet space.
- •Reflect on the things you love and are grateful for in your life.
- •List ten things you do when time in your free time. These are things you look forward to doing and would do them for free or even pay to do them. This list should include activities like "meditation" or "playing the guitar"
- Prioritize this list from most preferred to least preferred
- Write the top three activities on an index card and place the card somewhere that you will read it every day.
- •Spend at least 30 minutes doing one of these three activities every day for the next seven days.
- •Spend 10 minutes after the activity is over journaling about how you felt before and after doing the activity.

You may find that you feel energized or elevated following a 30-minute session of practicing your passion. This is completely normal. You can increase the time of your sessions if you feel inspired to continue. As you increase the amount of time you are doing your passion, you may start making subtle changes to your life that support a life style in which you can live your passion more naturally. I have a morning routine of chanting songs of love and gratitude when I wake up. This extraordinary practice has helped me start my days filled and surrounded by love and invites more positivity into my life. After 30 minutes of chanting songs of gratitude I find that I maintain an elevated mental state for the rest of my day by allowing my passion to be my touchstone of happiness.

CHAPTER 3

Devotion

"Devotion is the nectar that causes God to come looking for you."

- Swami Jaya Devi

DOES THE TITLE of this chapter scare you? Just stay with me for a moment ...

Like many of you, I do not believe that we need an organized religion in order to live a healthy and happy life, and in no way am I promoting or denouncing the beliefs of others. And yet... I have noticed that a connection to something outside of ourselves is often necessary to transcend a purely selfish existence, and that is what I am describing here when I speak of devotion.

I personally have had a rather jaded history with religion. I was forced like many children to go to my grandmother's church, and this became a place I tried desperately to escape every Sunday morning. Coming from my days of freedom living on the boat, I could not understand why anyone would want to sit inside and listen to a boring lecture instead of playing outside in the woods. As a result, I ran away from organized religion as soon as I was liberated from my grandmother's rules, not returning again until my mid-thirties.

It was my newly acquired gift of self-love that brought me back to my relationship with what I now call god. It was shortly after I allowed myself to love this concept called "god" that I realized the names and titles do not matter, it is all interconnected! Whatever your path has been up to now, please understand that this is not a chapter on religion but instead a chapter of selfless devotion.

True, the path of selflessness frequently takes place in the forest of organized religion. Many people thrive from a relationship with god and I have witnessed this relationship bring them to a space of community and love. There have also been severe disconnections in the name of religion, resulting in great human suffering, such as the Spanish inquisition or the Salem witch trials.

When I speak of devotion here, I am referring to the foundation of what we call "Zone 00" in the permaculture world. In permaculture, we design projects in spatial relationships. We then divide those spaces into zones based on the frequency of use. For instance, something you use every day (like a car) would be right outside your house, or in Zone 1. Zone 4 may have trees used for firewood or timber. We organize the system to maximize efficiency, which produces more abundance. Your home itself is typically called zone 0. This is where you will spend much of your time learning and socializing. Zone 00 is defined as all the thoughts, ideas, and actions that comprise who you are, also known as your heart or personality. Physical reflections of this Zone can be the particular way you respond to things and the words you say. Imagine, if you will, a movie projector. If your life is the movie, then the bulb creating the light would be your Zone 00.

During my 15-year career as a behavior analyst working with children with autism, I developed several tools to help organize and identify key factors that determine an individual's personality. I collected them and ranked them from most to least impactful and found that personal experience contributes the most in personality development. This includes how you were raised and any trauma or good fortune you may have encountered. If you took identical twins and separated them at birth, raised one in a den of thieves and the other in a royal court, you would find the resulting personalities to be very different.

We are all a product of the collected sum of our total experiences. Whatever you believe about the Nature versus Nurture debate, whether or not you believe in past lives or think that everything is just a random coincidence; your current reality is the collection of all of the thoughts and stories you label as the truth. Knowing this to be true, I am fascinated by the human potential for manifesting abundance. I have seen people change their lifestyles and actions instantly simply by exercising the miracle of free will.

We all have the ability to try and change any part of our lives at any time. This simple truth makes us all very powerful beings of creation. I am not saying that this is a magic trick and you can conjure things from thin air, instead, I am suggesting that what we believe helps to shape the world around us and I believe that we can achieve our wildest dreams in this life, but we have to first recognize our wildest dreams.

I went to college so that I could make money. I do not know why I wanted to make money but it was something I was told I needed to do. This led me to a life with plenty of money but no direction until one day I sat and thought about what I was here on this earth to do. I finally asked the question: What is my purpose here? This is when I heard my calling to help reconnect people to nature and help create abundance. Since that time, I have been invited to places all over the world to share this teaching, meeting thousands of people that share my dream of an interconnected world, and I have watched my life take a new direction. To find a genuine connection to your purpose in life and then putting that passion into action is the simplest way to begin on this path.

I do not think it is necessary to be religious for devotion to be present in our lives. Devotion can take form in many different ways. I have seen people devoted to caring for plants or making really good lasagna. The key concept I want to share with you is the importance of making something outside of your own personal desires important in your life. This practice creates activities in your life that greater than your own existence and become sacred. The amount of energy you give these sacred parts of your life will determine to what degree they will shape your future. This devotion will give your life direction.

Through technology, we are systematically removing some of the mystery and magic in life. It seems the further we progress in technology the more we are focused on the accuracy of our instruments and less with the purpose of the question. If you look at the culture of indigenous tribes, they are very familiar with living life deeply connected to nature. The Hopi people held their corn very sacred; they were devoted to nurturing the plants and respecting what they represented in their lives. The corn gives them food, they acknowledge it as their ancestors, and it defines their way of life. Every kernel is revered and honored. This adds power to the corn in the village and gives the community something to gather around. In modern society, we are losing this concept. We take our food and our relationships in our communities for granted. We are willingly trading a sacred way of life for one of separation and competition. When we devote ourselves to something greater than ourselves, we do things greater than ourselves.

One day, I opened my eyes after a meditation and I happened to be staring at a painting of a buddha with a glowing bubble surrounding his head. I realized this was his perception creating heaven all around himself. We all have the ability to carry this bliss bubble with us in our daily lives. We cannot control what happens to us, we can only control how we respond.

Our perception defines our life. For a skier on top of the mountain, heavy snow means a day full of excitement, adventure, and joy, but for the truck driver trying to get home to his family, that same snow means worry, frustration, and concern. When you can acknowledge the formlessness of perception and make conscious choices that create actions formed from clear thoughts in your own highest integrity, you will begin to change the world around you.

Integrity, or the lack thereof, can be defined by your true nature, or simply stated, what you do when no one is watching. We all have the ability to choose how we respond to life. The quality of our integrity increases when we choose to respond in a way that benefits all of nature. This includes the health of all plants, all animals, and all people. It's making the highest choice in the moment for the best outcome and, often, for the greater good. I believe that living a life rich in integrity is far more valuable than any financial wealth. Integrity will form your character and shape your relationships. When we become devoted to our integrity, we will begin to see the world as a reflection of this genuine and truthful space.

I feel blessed to have lived in an intentional, interfaith community named Sacred Kashi in Sebastian, Florida almost six years. It was here I really learned the importance of compassion and understanding. Each of the 80 residents were very different with their own beliefs and lifestyles. It took quite a bit of practice to live with patience and cooperation instead of the individually focused life I had been taught in school and in my cooperate life. I learned to give my time and energy to others and share their passion and beliefs.

I see people so concerned with "being right" that they do not take the time for compassion or understanding of other equally valid and sacred journeys and perspectives. When you devote yourself to compassion, you are freed from resentment and judgment. There is no race to the top of a particular mountain. We are all on our own paths. It is not our place to measure how spiritual we perceive our friends and family. There is no "sacred meter" that can measure spirituality that we can use to compare others. We are all on our own individual journey. I like to think we are 8 billion infinite beings creating our own personal worlds and sharing this planet together.

Imagine that the world is a spiral herb garden. The spiral herb garden has soil depths, water, and sunlight available at different spots in the spiral. Rosemary does well when supported by less water and more sun. If you place Rosemary at the top of the spiral, it is very likely it will grow well. If you were to place the Rosemary on the shady side on the bottom, the lack of sun and the excess of water would cause the plant to grow much more slowly. This is how I see us in our communities: If you thrive with sunshine and ocean air, a temperate mountain is not your perfect environment.

Thich Nhat Hanh has said, "When you plant lettuce, if it does not grow well, you don't blame the lettuce. You look for reasons it is not doing well. It may need fertilizer, or more water, or less sun. You never blame the lettuce."

One of the biggest challenges we face is to recognize the environment in which we personally thrive. It is not uncommon to see an individual suffer from medical conditions or emotional disorders that could simply be rectified by a change in climate. An individual may suffer a lifetime of unnecessary pain instead of simply re-planting themselves in a more optimal garden. I like to demonstrate this concept with a tool called the scales of permanence. PA Yeoman first developed the scales of permanence as a way of designing landscapes based on the difficulty of making changes within a system. We use the scales of permanence to determine how to place and cycle resources on a project depending on time and energy needs. The system includes a hierarchy of characteristics ranging from the hardest to easiest to change. These scales of permanence have been modified by many but my favorite rendition is by David Jacke and I will include it here:

Scales of Permanence:

- 1-Climate
- 2- Landform
- 3- Water
- 4- Access and circulation
- 5- Microclimates
- 6- Buildings and infrastructure
- 7- Zones of use
- 8- Soil
- 9- Aesthetics
- 10- Culture, Economic, Political, Spiritual

When I am doing a “life assessment” for an individual to design a life that creates abundance I use this same system with only a few changes. I still start with the top of the list, climate, as this is a very difficult thing to change. Are you a desert person or do you like the mountains? List the environments in which you feel best. There are no wrong answers, only your personal preference. I then use the answers to these questions to determine your perfect environment much in the same way as if I was trying to place a tropical plant in a landscape. I would consider the climate first. I would never put a coconut tree in the snow. The answers you have towards the bottom of the list are easier to change and slight changes could be made regardless of your setting such as the color of your house or what church you go to. This helps you focus on the things you can change in a more effective manner instead of spending energy trying to change things that are out of your control.

I suggest spending time connecting to your innermost wants and needs. Oftentimes, people spend more time reacting to events that appear in their lives than designing the events that happen and then consciously responding to them. When you have a strong mission or purpose in life to which you are devoted, you will choose more of the things that happen and play a very active role in shaping those events. If you do not pick a path, someone else may pick one for you, usually to serve his or her agenda. Meditation is a wonderful practice in gaining clarity on this point of focus. I have met many people who believe the purpose of meditation is to feel good or at peace. While meditation can serve this purpose, I do not agree that this is the goal. I believe the purpose of meditation is to be able to gain a clear perspective by quieting the mind and being able to do the right thing in the moment.

If you are on a sailboat in the middle of a hurricane you need to be present in the moment, clearly focused on what actions are going to help you navigate safely through the storm. If the wind gusts, you will need to be present and have the awareness to let out the main sail so the boat does not get knocked down. Most people do not think of an intense moment like this when they think of the benefits of meditation. In challenging and perilous situations, a background in meditation can help you focus energy in the right place and free yourself from paralyzing fear or distractions. The more you practice this focus, the more you will be able to utilize this cultivated skill in life's most challenging moments, The more you focus on your life's mission, the clearer it will become for you, which will shape the actions you initiate, which will shape the interactions you have, which will produce many of the opportunities and relationships you experience.

This is how simple meditation can help produce a life of abundance and happiness. There is no guarantee that if you meditate you will live a life of abundance. There is no simple road map to reach a desired destination of happiness. Instead the journey becomes the destination. As you learn to look at each day as an opportunity to learn and grow, you will start to change the way you respond to the challenges you find along the way. Permaculture reflects this idea as well. I do not look at Permaculture as a way of doing things, instead, I see Permaculture as a holistic way to think about things. The more I adopt the regenerative paradigm of Permaculture with all of the elements within my life, interconnected in a beautiful thriving system moving with all the other interconnected systems, the more I truly appreciate the value of mindfulness and presence.

I personally enjoy when I recognize the golden thread of truth woven between different ideologies. When I see yoga, Christians, permaculture, Zen meditation, and countless spiritual leaders with similar teachings, I listen deeply and appreciate the message. I cannot personally recommend any one way for you to follow as this would be discrediting all of the others. It is a personal choice from whom you seek guidance on your journey. I will say that I hope whichever way you choose will lead you to abundance, connection, happiness, and joy.

Activity 2:
Sit Spot

A sit spot is simply a place in nature that you visit regularly to cultivate awareness as you observe and study the patterns of local plants and animals, as you become a living part of the ecosystem. Technology has an associated disconnection from nature and has taken us away from our wild origins. This exercise can reintroduce you to this orchestra of interconnected life all around us.

The activity will take 25 minutes and we ask you devote every day for one week to get started. Consistency is important when introducing the sit spot into your daily routine. Be sure you schedule a time when you will not be tempted to use your phone or visitors will not interrupt you.

- Pick a spot, preferably outdoors, to which you feel attracted. This could be a river, bench, or front porch. Consider the possibility of rain when you make your decision.
- Go to this same spot every day and at the same time each day.
- Simply observe and be present. Notice the wind, sun, and wildlife in the area. Do not have an agenda, just observe.
- After sitting for 15 minutes or more, journal for 10 minutes about what came up internally and what you saw around you. How are things different from yesterday? How are they the same?

You will begin to notice the changes that occur with the inhabitants of your spot overtime and how you personally interact with each of them. Feel free to continue this practice after the week is over. I personally use this activity often as a method to reintroduce myself to the ecosystem around me. As we increase the time we send in this state of connection, we begin to remember our natural state of peace and realize a calm that supports us.

CHAPTER 4

Freedom

"Don't ask what the world needs.
Ask what makes you come alive, and go do it.
Because what the world needs is people who have come alive."

- Howard Thurman

I HAVE HAD MANY JOBS in my life. My first job was as a dishwasher in a seafood restaurant in Melbourne, Florida. I learned many lessons about the foodservice industry there. One of the things I learned was how much they like to celebrate after work. We would serve lobsters to people by day and shots to each other at night. This was a very fuzzy time in my life but I remember this job was the perfect launching pad to begin my search for personal freedom. It was here that I first learned that people tend to label you by the job you hold. I thought how odd it was that people categorize a person's identity into neat little titles like, "John the teacher," or "Mary the doctor," and I remember thinking that individually we are so much more than limited titles. I was washing dishes for a paycheck but I did not identify as a dishwasher. I wanted to help make the planet healthy and heal our ecosystem, so I thought of myself as more of a planet doctor than a dishwasher.

I began to ask myself, "If our true passion is not identified by the jobs we have, why do we do the things we do or act the way we act?" I began to realize that we are born with the freedom to make choices that directly shape how we live our lives every day. If we want to stop watching television or begin to eat only organic food, we have control over those choices. We all have the freedom to choose who we are and what we do.

I began to take more time to appreciate personal freedom. Personal freedom can inspire people to pursue their dreams and accomplish their goals. I acknowledge the fact that I am blessed with an abundance of various forms of wealth, some of which has been handed to me and some is the result of personal choices. As an example, as I was writing this book, I was exploring the northeast mountains of New Hampshire. The environment there filled my spirit with inspiration and helped me get into a place of creativity and expressiveness so I could write a quality book to the best of my ability.

It took a tremendous amount of multi-faceted wealth, including opportunity, to make this happen. First, our country had to have the roads and infrastructure for such a journey to take place. Second, I needed personal wealth in the form of a car and gas to fuel the trip. Third, I had to make choices to create the opportunity to take three months off from work. Finally, I needed a wealth of confidence and courage to follow my dream to write this book and go against the mainstream life.

Such forms and combinations of wealth do not guarantee freedom, but lack of wealth can certainly limit the choices and possibilities. Without a car and roads, I would not have had the freedom to make the trip. Or, I could have had the same amount of tangible wealth but not the courage to start the journey. I see freedom expressed as what we choose to do with the situations we face in this life.

I will now go deeper into why freedom is so important and how it plays such an active role in helping create healthy and happy humans.

Humans are the only animals on earth who go to work. Most every animal performs activities during their day such as hunting, building, or finding a mate, but humans are the only ones that put it in a category and call it "work."

According to a 2017 Gallup poll, 85% of people worldwide hate their jobs. Many see those jobs as a source of frustration and stress. This results in an unfulfilled existence where they feel the need to get away, either on an expensive vacation or nightly, in front of a television set. The average person will spend a total of 13 years and 2 months of their lives working. Because we will spend so much time working, we should choose a job that gives us joy and happiness, right?

The system that has become modern-day normal is designed to keep us working those jobs that 85 percent of us do not like. It starts with training us early by forcing us to get up and go to school, learning curricula that has little to do with human development or natural survival, then maybe work through college or perhaps a trade school, then going to a job you don't like, all so you can work your way up the ladder to a position of power and retire at age 65 or 70. Typically, there are not many considerations for happiness or feeling fulfilled in this job. I do not see this as a effective recipe for happy and healthy humans.

Because we spend so much time at work, we should take the time to choose the work we do very carefully. I think of the times of blacksmiths and bards, where people would spend their entire lives perfecting their crafts. Their jobs were an expression of their passion. Could this be achieved today by everyone? What if we all could find a way for our skills to benefit our communities and express them with true passion?

I am as excited to go to work every day and help people find their connection to the natural world. It fills my heart with happiness and purpose. I have found a job that I enjoy so much that it is the reason I jump out of bed in the morning.

The authors of "The Millionaire Next Door" state that only 18 percent of Americans were self-employed. However, this 18 percent was four times more likely to be millionaires. I believe one reason for this is the self-employed may have more freedom to choose the work they do and they choose work they are passionate about.

Another contributing component of freedom is simplicity. I love to say there are two ways to get rich: make more or use less. We live in a time with so many material possessions around us that it is easy to forget what is truly important to us. These possessions create situations in which we must protect them with our precious time and money. They eventually limit our freedom to live in the moment as free and unattached humans.

In 2001 my father bought an RV and drove to Alaska. This had been a dream of his for many years. He did not have much room in the RV so he had to consider every possession very carefully. After his decision he had a few material possessions he couldn't fit in his new home on wheels and asked if I wanted them. I had already begun simplifying my life and refused, so he hired a storage unit. He traveled to Alaska and paid for that storage unit for five years. When he returned, he asked if I would help him clear out the storage unit and I watched as he looked around at all the stuff he couldn't throw away years before. There were old pots and pans, furniture, and a novelty singing bass. He ended up taking most of it to the dump. He hadn't let go of these things earlier because they were so important to him, but when he returned from Alaska, he realized that he didn't even recognize them.

The more simply we live our lives, the clearer it can become. Finding the value in the sunrise and in the health of your community can become your greatest currency and can replace the need for fancy material possessions. When we begin to appreciate all the little things around us, we start to need fewer material possessions to give us feelings of purpose. We begin to realize that these feelings of peace can only exist within us.

Simplicity will also lead us into the world of regenerative lifestyles. Solar energy, rainwater catchment, and composting toilets are all examples of systems that are simple and create a direct connection with our ecosystem. Whether you are in the city or a rural farmhouse, a lifestyle with all of its components connected will use fewer resources and create less waste.

The composting toilet, for example, saves water and doesn't require expensive plumbing or waste treatment plants. It also results in high-quality fertilizer that can feed fruit trees and perennial food forests. This system results in lower inputs and higher yields than a conventional bathroom. The result of this regenerative system is more free time to spend with your family because you are not working to pay for the expensive plumbing system and you have delicious organic food to eat from your garden with a cleaner and healthier earth to live upon.

The more of these regenerative systems we have in our lives, the more our local communities will thrive by using fewer resources to produce a higher quality of living.

While I was visiting an off-grid village in New Zealand, I noticed a family who made their own bread. Truly, it was the most delicious bread I have ever had eaten. Each day they would mix the dough, let it rise, and then bake it. It took perhaps 20 minutes out of the day. As I was enjoying this amazing loaf, I began to wonder why everyone doesn't do this. It was so much better than even the finest bread you could buy in the stores. I convinced myself it was for convenience. I then thought of getting into my car, driving to the store, getting the bread wrapped in plastic from the shelf, standing in line to pay for it with money I had worked for, and driving back home, and I realized that it was actually less convenient than baking the bread myself. The fresh bread was cheaper, needed no plastic or petroleum to produce, and tasted better.

In a consumerist society, we learn that doing things ourselves is harder and not worth the time, so we hire others who will probably not put the same love into it. It is sold as being easier and cheaper but the hidden costs are to the environment and to the quality of the product. When we hire the person that charges the lowest price, they may sacrifice quality to get the job. This is how we have traded quality for convenience.

We built an off-grid eco-village at Sustainable Kashi with regenerative food, water, and energy systems. This demonstration site was designed to show people how easy and rewarding a life connected to our perfect planet can be. We harvested our own food from the gardens, collected our energy from solar and tidal collectors, and lived in community helping each other grow stronger together. I feel it is so much easier to do something you have seen done successfully but I have seen far more examples of how to start a fast food franchise than how to start a regenerative community.

There is a story of a man who drives to work every day. On his way, there's a pothole that repeatedly causes damage to his tire, so he spends his life getting the tire fix and replaced, never once thinking about fixing the pothole. This is how I see modern society's mindset. We get jobs that pay well so we can afford to retire with security but those same jobs fill our lives with stress and anxiety. Perhaps if we were not so focused on the future or what other people thought, we would be open to the infinite possibilities life has to offer each of us in this present moment.

The real foundation of freedom lives in the mind. If you are in prison or living with limited access to food or shelter, then it will be very difficult for you to feel free. I have met people who have plenty of material resources however still believe they do not have many choices in their lifestyle. I witness them believe they have to do things they don't want to do in order to "get by". This belief system is often rooted in fear and scarcity and is a significant cause of separation, stress, and anxiety. When we take away the things in our life that we "have" to do, the things that really matter to us become clearer.

I first traveled to Costa Rica when I was 18 years old. I threw a backpack on and jumped on a plane. I did not have an itinerary or an agenda; I just wanted to see the country. When I got there, I met travelers from around the world. I noticed that the American travelers were only able to stay for a week or two and European travelers were there for several months. I noticed the Americans believed it was strange to travel for so long and the Europeans thought it was strange to travel so briefly. This is when I started to realize that what we consider "normal" was all in our minds.

The mind is the source of our perception and how we view everything in our lives. Most of us are trained at a very early age by our parents and schools to behave within certain norms. This system creates a more productive society with fewer social problems but limits individuality and free thought. You can see many examples of this in history but one of my favorites is that of Socrates. Socrates was an ancient Greek philosopher considered to be the main source of Western thought and was condemned to death for his Socratic method of questioning. Socrates pointed out that human choice was motivated by the desire for happiness. He stated that ultimate wisdom comes from knowing oneself and the more a person knows, the greater his or her ability to reason and make choices that will bring true happiness. To train the mind to see things clearly without illusions has been the purpose of meditation and countless enlightening practices throughout history. We have created a world based on competition, and competition does have its place in nature. However, we have the ability to help each other and live in a cooperative society. We can build each other up and as we begin to see the best in people, and see the proverbial glass as half full, we begin to create opportunities and situations where they might not have revealed themselves before. I believe this is the greatest form of freedom we can experience in this life.

Imagine yourself as a leaf floating down a river. The leaf does not fight or compete against the current but simply flows with the water. To relax and surrender into the flow of life and allow everything to unfold naturally can be extremely challenging. We can get so caught up with how we think everything should be that we can forget to remember the natural flow of the river.

As you practice living without these expectations, you can begin to let go of the things that do not create happiness in your life. Every month I walk around my home and look for things that I have not used or no longer have value to me. Living on a small sailboat, this does not take very long. This includes clothes I have not worn, books I have not read, and things just taking up space in my life. I give away the things I cannot justify keeping in my life to people who need them. This exercise has many benefits. Joy fills those receiving the gifts, lifts their spirits, and creates positivity in their world. The space created by letting the items go creates fertile ground for things I am trying to manifest toward my life's purpose to appear. The ability to be detached from the way I think things should be or by the people around me is an effective tool in achieving personal freedom. This is not to say that you do not care about the people around you, only that you are not attached to the role they play in your life. You appreciate them in whatever way they choose to show up and are not bound by any expectations of their behavior. We cannot control others' behavior and I have personally witnessed the belief that we can create many arguments and instill rage leading to disappointment and resentment. Letting go of everything that does not fill your life with happiness gives space to the things that can.

Freedom is a gift we are all born with. We do not have control over all of life's situations, but we can cultivate control over how we respond to them. We all have freedom of choice to approach challenges with patience, kindness, compassion, and love. The more we choose to embody these qualities and respond in these ways, the more our lives can reflect the abundant beauty that is all around us.

Activity 3:
Create a Functional Analysis for your Life

A functional analysis is a tool used to examine a system by identifying the elements it needs in order to thrive and the results the system creates. By identifying the needs and yields of one system, we can simply connect related systems together creating a more efficient and abundant integrated ecosystem.

- Pick a spot, preferably outdoors, and use the list of activities from activity 1 for this activity. This list will include the three activities you selected that you have been doing.
- Take a second to think about these things and write a narrative as to why you enjoy them. What do you get out of engaging in them? For example, I love to garden because I enjoy eating organic food, spending time in nature, and digging in the dirt with friends.
- Write one narrative for each of the three activities you have identified.
- After you complete the list, make two columns on a piece of paper. Label one column "Needs" and label the other column "Yields."
- Examine your narrative and fill in each column with the appropriate description that the activity on your narrative list "Need" in one column and what they "Yield" in the other column.

You will use this list as a tool in designing your new life of abundance so make sure you store it in a safe place. As you start to see the things in your life that you want and need, you can identify the things that you do not want. Great work, we will go further with this activity in the next chapter!

CHAPTER 5

Forgiveness and Joy

"Sometimes your joy is the source of your smile,
but sometimes your smile can be the source of your joy."

- Thich Nhat Hanh

ONE OF THE ESSENTIAL facets of my life is the magnitude and the consistency of the joy I experience. Where is the value if I have all the money in the world or live my wildest dreams if my soul is not filled with joy?

The quality and intensity of the joy you feel will shape the events you experience and the people that surround you. It will determine the people who choose to spend time with you because energy triggers similar energy. If you play a low note "A" on a piano, every note "A" on that piano will vibrate on the octaves above and below. The original frequency triggers similar frequencies through the entire spectrum of sound. Now imagine that the note you play is a simple act of kindness. When you do a simple act of kindness it triggers similar acts of kindness all around you. When you find yourself in a genuine joyful state of being, it gives others around you permission to feel a similar sense of joy and express it. Imagine that all feelings have a vibrational frequency and that every emotion you have radiates into the world. Which vibration would you choose to add? Most of us would choose to add a pleasant feeling like happiness or peace.

However, life will deliver difficulties for us all and it is easy to take those challenges personally and become jaded and cold to others out of fear of being hurt again. When we face new situations with fear from an old experience, we recreate that same negative situation and this becomes a loop that can be very difficult to escape. It takes courage to face the world with an open heart after being hurt, but if you choose to focus on the pain, you will be surrounded by pain.

When my mother left us on the boat when I was two years old, I held onto that pain for a very long time. This affected all my relationships, especially those with women. There was fear of abandonment and feelings of not being loved in all my romantic relationships. This old scar had burned its way deeply into my life and I could not seem to get away from it.

Our instructor shared a beautiful exercise during my first yoga teacher training course. She led us through a guided meditation where we visualized the person who caused us the most pain. Everyone's pain was different and everyone had a different person emerge in their mind. For me it was my mother. How could she leave a two-year-old child? How could she just choose not to be my mom anymore? So, I visualized her in front of me looking cruel and heartless and I hated her. We were then asked to see them as if they were only six years old. This was difficult for me at first but I surrendered to the exercise. I saw this woman who caused me so much pain as a sweet little girl laughing and I just felt the pain evaporate. How could I be angry at a child? We ended the exercise by hugging the child and filling them with forgiveness. This powerful exercise not only helped me learn how to let go of resentment toward my mother but also led me to the path of forgiveness for everyone who had caused me pain. It is said that forgiving someone is like letting someone out of jail, and then realizing that that someone is you. Releasing the poison of resentment will lead you to joy in your life and in the lives of those around you.

One of the hardest challenges when practicing forgiveness is forgiving yourself. Everyone has made terrible mistakes. Trust me, I am an expert at making terrible mistakes. It is important to be gentle with yourself and forgive yourself as you move through these lessons in life. Let go of any disappointment, frustration, anxiety, guilt, and shame that the mistake might have created. Allow yourself to learn from the lesson and grow from the experience. Be thankful for the opportunity for this lesson and make an effort not to repeat the same mistake. Instead of being angry at myself for making a mistake, I appreciate that I still have more to learn. This is the magic of the human experience we all share—and humility helps us get back up and try again.

I do not want to give the illusion that once you start living with love, gratitude, and forgiveness that joy will just start flowing into your life and everything will be rainbows and puppies all day long. We are all still human and there will still be challenges in our lives that we must face.

Instead, I want to introduce the notion that facing these challenges with a perspective based in love, gratitude, forgiveness can greatly increase your quality of life. Perhaps you will show the person who cut you off in traffic forgiveness or you notice you have more patience to wait in line at the DMV after doing a 30-minute meditation each morning. These effects will begin to magnify the positivity you experience in your life and add to your life of abundance. As these positive experiences start to increase, you will begin to feel happier and healthier.

We like to utilize the edge of ecosystems in permaculture. This is because there is more diversity and fertility on the edge of an ecosystem. Picture yourself at the beach. The fish who live in the ocean cannot live on the sand and the people on the beach cannot live under the water. There are different sets of plants and animals in the ocean and on land. Between the two are the tide pools with yet another distinct set of life forms. There you will find sea cucumbers, welks, and urchins. In this edge you will find more life than in similarly sized areas of the other two zones. When we think of the phrase "living on the edge," we think of someone who creates motion in their life. Energy wants to move through a system. The edge is where energy from one system can transform into energy in the next. Energy kept in one place creates stagnation. We see this in water cisterns, batteries, and even in the human experience. If we create stagnation in our lives by not engaging in new and challenging situations, then we become stuck in that stale energy and feel unaccomplished and empty. This usually stems from fear of failure or discomfort. The results are feelings of monotony, depression, and boredom. I suggest that it is better to have failed at attempting to do the things you love than never to have tried to do those things at all. You do not have to be successful to feel the joy in your passion. You can feel joy by simply taking a chance and getting out of your comfort zone.

As you start to take more chances and add more adventure (whether internal or external) into your life, you may see that the opportunities you are presented with may increase. I have seen people who were living mundane lives leap into quests that would make any knight of the Round Table envious and watched as their life transformed into an adventure. Once you have identified your passion and begin to share it with everyone around you, you have begun raising the collective vibrations of the entire universe. How many times have you sat and had conversations about politics, television, what horrible things your co-workers did, or what else is wrong in the world? This culture of negative interaction has been accepted by society and normalized. When we vibrate at this level, that's what we attract. It's what resonates back to us. It becomes our new normal.

Now picture yourself conversing instead about what fills your heart with joy and having everyone share their feelings of hope. Picture yourself sharing your dreams with your friends and family and talking about the greatness in each other. Your conversations are about achieving your goals and supporting each other. Which scenario feels better and creates more opportunities for growth in your life?

This shift in what is currently "normal" has to occur. There is a modern trend toward accepting new negative social norms and abandoning what has been established as normal and healthy previously based on biology and evolution. Take the example of breastfeeding. Humans have evolved to be able to nurture our young offspring with this amazing ability to produce milk and until the last hundred years it was seen as completely normal. Recently, with the addition of social embarrassment and sexual shame, breastfeeding has been turned into an act that should only be done privately, hidden from our communities. This goes against our biological evolution. The same thing is happening with our social interactions and in our connection to nature. We must collectively stop accepting these new standards of normal which often lead to isolation and separation. We must come together and remember that we are here to feel joy together, sharing the beauty of this world.

Systems in nature are very good at sharing resources. Imagine a forest with old-growth trees. The trees take what they need in order to make new leaves and grow. Then the trees will drop those leaves and all their old branches. That detritus (leaf litter) collects on the forest floor and starts to decompose. This acts as a blanket for millions of microorganisms and fungi. The microorganisms create more fertility by adding nitrogen and moisture and the fungi act as a highway for these nutrients to spread throughout the forest. Nature depends on sharing for survival.

Permaculture uses biomimicry to imitate the patterns of nature to create successful and abundant systems. Biomimicry is an intrinsic concept in Permaculture. Through observing millions of years of evolution, we learn from the process and utilize nature's wisdom in our designs. Scientists today are using biomimicry to develop more efficient technology. Photovoltaic cells that resemble the leaves of plants and LED emitters that imitate fireflies are just two examples of using nature as a roadmap to creating more efficient technology.

An example of using biomimicry in a social situation is tool sharing to increase the abundance of a community. The practice is easy and looks much like a public library but instead of books there are belt sanders and screwdrivers. The idea that every home should have its own lawn mower is based on isolationism and separatism. If a community can agree to a use schedule that meets everyone's needs and can also agree to keep all the tools accounted for and in good working order, then the system is more efficient than individual ownership and the community grows more resilient.

In contrast, as we travel further away from our connection to nature, we are experiencing more repercussions. In 2005 Richard Louv introduced the term NDD or nature deficit disorder. This concept defines a disconnection with nature, especially in children, resulting in diminished use of the senses, attention difficulties, conditions of obesity, and higher rates of emotional and physical illnesses. Humans are part of the natural world. As we disconnect ourselves from nature's patterns, we are seeing a decrease in our personal satisfaction and joy.

My brother died in a car accident when I was 35 years old. He had battled alcoholism most of his life and swerved off the road one early February morning. He had a wife and a daughter but he could never find joy in his life. I remember talking to him and he would ask me why I was so happy. My brother owned a construction company and was making lots of money. I was in college working in the student library making less than $10,000 a year. He had boats, cars, and all the material things he could ever want.

He could not understand why I was filled with joy every day and he was filled with emptiness. I asked him to walk with me in the woods. I tried to explain to him that my joy was given to me by the beautiful simplicity of the forest. I tried to explain how nature gave me everything I ever needed. The wind on my face, the grass under my feet, the birds singing above me are gifts of nature and they are always around me. I thought that if I could get him into nature that he could feel these gifts as well.

We never took that walk. I now see alcoholism, drug use, and many other addictions as a result of humanity walking away from a deep connection with nature and into an existence that is isolated and empty. Our connection with nature heals. A 2018 study in the Journal of Gerontology states that ICU rooms with windows result in shorter hospital stays for patients. The simple addition of a view of nature creates an environment that is more conducive to better sleep and a decrease in stress. This can also be seen in the workplace with employee productivity and overall satisfaction if the offices have windows looking out on nature.

Most of us are born into a world of joy. If you look into the eyes of a child you may see the amazement and wonder that their gift of innocent curiosity brings. As we become culturally processed and experience challenges in life, we slowly lose that innocence and often become more jaded and colder. We begin to close ourselves to others out of fear of pain and this creates a cycle that leads to isolation. We must learn to balance the beauty of the child's mind and the wisdom we find through our experiences in order to find our greatest personal happiness. If we lose our sense of wonder, it can lead to a sense of hopelessness and we may not try new things out of fear of making mistakes or wasting time. If we get stuck in our logic and intelligence, we can become stale and mundane. Balance is the key.

Forgiveness and joy are forever interconnected. It is hard to have joy when we are poisoned by resentment for others or ourselves and it is hard to forgive when we are not able to find joy in our lives. These two aspects strengthen each other. Allow yourself to truly forgive the past. Allow joy to be an integral part of your life. I believe we are here to experience forgiveness joy and if we live with integrity and learn to live our passion then every second of our lives can have great purpose. Time is a gift that has been given to us. Spend some time finding ways to provide a method of expressing this purpose and putting your passions into action. As you begin to feel the excitement of manifesting this state of being, your life may become filled with more joy than you ever thought possible.

Activity 4:
Create Joy and Give Comfort

You will need 5-10 friends that have each completed the functional analysis from activity three, 10 small pieces of paper for every person, and something to write with for this activity.

- Gather with five friends with the Functional Analysis that each of you have completed from Chapter 4.
- Write the five things from your "Need" list you created in activity three each on their own piece of paper. These needs should be meaningful to you and important elements needed in achieving happiness in your life.
- Next write five things from your "Yield" list you created in activity three each on their own piece of paper. These should be the things you "harvest" from living a happy and productive life.
- Spend the next 30 minutes matching your yields with other people's needs.
- Allow this activity to create conversations and observe how these elements are connected between you and your friends.
- Write down the newly discovered network that you have uncovered. Make sure to write down whom each connection is with and what the exchanges take place.

This exercise can lead to productive community relationships that are mutually beneficial. This can be the seed for private economies and local exchanges to actualize and sprout. The more we interact and share our needs and our gifts with each other, the more resilient and connected we become as a community.

CHAPTER 6

Creation

"All that we are arises with our thoughts. With our thoughts, we make the world."

- Buddha

I HEARD IT SAID that humans are the seeds that replant the Garden of Eden. I ignored these words when I first heard them because of my aversion to organized religion but I can now see the truth in them. We are all infinite creatures of creation sitting right in the middle of our own personal universe. Most of us do not realize that we are the creators and instead believe that we are just reacting to the chaos of the world around. The amazing thing is that whether you believe you are creating this world or that you are just reacting to the world around you, you are right. I like to imagine we are playing a game of "go fish" with the universe and we ask for all the "cards" we want to experience. We may ask "Do you have any pain?" and the universe provides. "Do you have true love?" and in walks romance. The world can be a cage or a playground. It is a marvelous day when we realize we can ask for love and abundance just as easily as we can ask for suffering.

One of my favorite activities is taking long walks in the woods. I enjoy the activity because I feel connected when I am deep in the forest. I see the towering trees above me and crawling insects below my feet and I feel part of the on-going symphony of life. I have enjoyed hiking most of my life. When I was younger, I remember everything merging into one big forest with not much detail. I have since learned many of the scientific names for the plants and animals in the forest. Now I label each of the edible plants I see and list their medicinal uses in my mind just for fun. I identify the mushrooms growing on a decomposing log. I remember the migratory patterns of the birds I see flying overhead. The truly amazing thing is that all these things were happening before I ever knew what they were. The mushrooms were still growing and the birds were still migrating but I was not aware of them and therefore they did not exist in my universe.

You can see the same phenomenon when you buy a new car and then start to see that same car on your way to work every day. It's amazing to realize that the car was there before you bought yours; you just did not see it. This is also true for love and abundance. They are all around you right now. If you choose to focus on fear or on things that you do not want to happen to you, then these are the things that you will see and recognize every day. We can choose to polish or smudge the glass that we see the world through.

I was living in Honolulu, Hawaii in 2007. I wanted to create a farm using these new tools of manifestation I had recently found. I began to look for land on the Hawaiian island and the cheapest I could find was an old pineapple farm with toxic soil for 5 million dollars. I decided that the amount of time I would have to work in order to afford the land would not leave much time to build the farm of my dreams or live the life of abundance I was seeking. I had recently learned to be non-attached to how things will look so I moved back to Florida to begin construction on a 5-acre plot on the Econlockhatchee River in Orlando. The land was perfect because of its natural beauty and it was 30 minutes outside of Orlando, creating a nice buffer from the city. I decided to dive deep into my new life of manifesting anything I wanted: I designed a fantastic log cabin that sat on 8-foot concrete pillars because I had always dreamed of living in a tree house as a child. I started the project by building a temporary homestead in the woods behind the site of my new cabin. I built a composting toilet, an outdoor kitchen, and a place to get away from the bugs and the Florida sun.

I lived in this off-grid eco-village for 442 days. Friends would come and visit and help build the cabin. We would sing songs at night around the campfire. We were a community, a tribe. When the house was completed, I remember thinking I liked my life so much that I would rather remain in my simple tent in the woods than move into this log cabin in the sky. But as the next Florida summer arrived, I left my forested paradise and I moved into the cabin.

I designed it to be a demonstration site for alternative technology so that people could see these amazing energy-saving features in action. The home had organic gardens, solar panels, water catchment systems, and many other environmentally friendly qualities to help simplify and redesign the way we live. In 2008 the house caught the attention of Oprah Magazine and was featured in an article called "Back to Basics." This article includes two families that decided to voluntarily simplify their lives.

To afford spending so long building an energy efficient log cabin, I had to give up many of the comforts of modern society. I did not have air conditioning or cable TV. My nightly entertainment was playing music and talking to my local community. My days included watering the gardens, feeding the chickens, and building my home. I quickly discovered that this life of simplicity was far more rewarding than any other I had known. It became clear to me that what we focus our attention on becomes our lives.

If we choose to search for money or corporate success, our time will be filled with board meetings and conversations about finances. My days were filled with conversations about nature, community, and making the world a more abundant playground for future generations. The more I let go of the paradigm of corporate America, the more my life was filled with people who shared my thoughts and beliefs. It became easier for me to believe I could create the life of my dreams.

There is a term in positive psychology known as the flow state. Mihály Csíkszentmihályi has defined it as an optimal state of consciousness where we feel our best and perform our best. When we enter the flow state, things become easier. As a musician, you can think of this as being "in the pocket." As an athlete, you can think of the flow state as being "in the zone." An important concept to understand is that in this flow state we become completely enveloped by our passion. Nothing else seems to matter. We become more effective and more driven to accomplish our goals.

My first realization that I was in a flow state was during the construction of the log cabin. I would work 15-hour days and want to work more but ran out of day light. I would use a solar powered light to keep working in the darkness. I believed so much in what I was doing and I was enjoying every second of the process that I never considered things like how much money I could be making or what I was going to do after work. The simplest way to enter the flow state is by finding ways of putting your love into action every day of your lives. What would you do if you could do anything?

I have enjoyed going to drum circles for many years. If you've never been to one, this is where people play drums together in celebration, usually in a circle. They dance, give praise, and elevate their consciousness together. I have seen many people enter into this state of bliss at a drum circle. I now recognize this as the flow state. Each individual who achieves this flow state can join other people around them who have also achieved this heightened state of consciousness, raising the collective vibration of the group. When conscious people gather together with a common goal, the energy can grow exponentially. I remember seeing people walk up to drum circles and watching their hearts immediately open. That is the power of heightened collective consciousness. We can use this power to create communities of cooperation, love, and abundance.

Permaculture has many concepts for designing and creating abundance systems. I will discuss two that I have found helpful in creating a life of abundance, known as zones and sectors.

Zones are ways of separating areas based on location, resources, and frequency of use. When we separate an area into zones, we increase the likeliness of them being maintained and therefore increase the productivity of the areas. Typically, there are five zones in a complete Permaculture design, but it is not necessary to include all five in every design.

Zone 5 is left untouched and is used as an example of how the natural ecosystem of an area operates. This is a space to cultivate biodiversity simply by doing nothing. When I am doing a new design, I always look to zone five for examples and ideas of what type of systems will work best in an area.

Zone 4 is typically used as a border forest. This can be a place for sustainable agriculture such as timber or firewood production. There are not very many inputs required in this area, nor does it need to be visited very often.

Zone 3 contains areas that need slightly more attention. This area may include self-fed animals and hardy seasonal crops such as bamboo, corn, or wheat.

Zone 2 will usually contain systems that require daily attention. This could include chickens and more tender crops that need to be harvested and checked daily.

Zone 1 requires frequent observation. This includes plants we eat every day and things we want to see every day, such as flowers, water features, and things that bring us happiness.

Zone 0 is our home and where we spend most of our time. We could have sprouts and ferments in this area, as well as a space for learning, such as the library or a classroom. This is where you recharge your batteries- both literally and figuratively.

Zone 00 is a way of expressing what is within our hearts. Everything we create is a reflection of this zone. I often say that every garden will fail if the garden within your heart is not maintained. Zone 00 is where all the seeds of creation are planted. Why you think the thoughts you do and the actions you choose are all born in this space.

I was able to see many examples of this with the interns during my time at Sustainable Kashi. They come with their tent, sleeping bag, and all the personal belongings they believe are important to stay for three weeks on a 10 x 10 wooden platform in an off-grid eco-village. During these three weeks, I see the area around these platforms transform. I watch these spaces change into a reflection of the individual's Zone 00. I have seen areas with candy wrappers or other small pieces of trash around them and I have seen areas with art and flowers arrive beautifully around them like altars. This is truly an amazing process to watch. Each person has his or her own unique impact on the environment. I have even seen the plants that grow around an area change, depending on the person staying on the site. The physical appearance of a person's living space is a direct reflection of their thoughts and feelings.

These zones are not just imaginary borders on a piece of property, but instead, they can be the framework used when designing a life of abundance. Let's take an example of a woman who loves to surf. If she loves to surf and is happiest when she does it every day, she should not live in the mountains. The amount of time and energy it would take to travel to the ocean would not result in a system of abundance. If it takes 2 hours and a tank of gas to drive to the beach, this is valuable time she is spending not doing what she loves. It is important to design our lives so the results of our time and energy feed our passions, creating abundance. Her Zone 0 is in the wrong place. If she lived at the beach, she could give surf lessons, making money doing what she enjoys, using the time that she would be driving if she were still living in the mountains. We need a clear assessment of what makes us happy and what we need to thrive so we may design our lives to most effectively create this reality. The better our lives are designed, the easier it will be for us to maintain the health and abundance of the entire system.

The next Permaculture tool I want to share with you is called sectors. Sectors are simply defined as the way energy moves through a property. This can include prevailing winds, wildlife, seasonal temperatures, elevation, and even things such as noise or a beautiful view. The idea is to capture energy from one system to fuel other systems that you have created.

If you have a ridge that funnels large amounts of wind, you may find that this would be a good setting for a turbine to capture that energy and transform it into electricity. The more energy we can capture from existing components of a system and utilize reduces the amount of energy we have to import from other non-renewable sources. This gives us a smaller environmental footprint, which can reduce the amount of waste we produce, as well as saves us money!

Drawing sectors onto a map of your property is a great way to see how the yields from one system can feed the needs of another. On our farm, we have a need for mulch in the intensive garden beds. This would cost hundreds of dollars if we had to purchase this mulch from feed stores. Instead, we use bamboo leaves, which were planted as windbreaks on our property. The bamboo protects our food forest in the winter from the north winds and the leaves that drop year-round are high in silica and make a wonderful addition to our soil. The more we can utilize the energy found on our property, the less inputs will be required for the system to be abundant.

We can use this sector map to help create a life of abundance. If you can label how energy is moving through your life, you can utilize this energy to feed other parts of your life, creating abundance. I saw a wonderful example of this in New Zealand in a town called Raglan. They have a program called Xtreme Zero Waste (http://xtremezerowaste.org.nz) that takes what people throw away, strips it down, and repackage it into useful components. They sell these components in a storefront creating thousands of dollars in profits. They also divert massive amounts of trash from the landfill. This results in an abundant system in a city with 75% diversion from the landfill all because they learned to capture the energy moving through the system. When we cycle resources through a system, this creates abundance.

I personally enjoy traveling, teaching people how to connect with our ecosystem, and living with people that share my beliefs. This is what I have defined as being important for me to live an abundant and happy existence. I have designed a life where I can teach people all over the globe how to live lives of abundance and create community. Each part of my life feeds another, creating an overflow of energy that I can share with my students, family, and friends.

We are all creating our realities whether we know it or not. We have all had many difficult challenges. When I was young, I would avoid the challenges and simply move on to something not so difficult. This resulted in lots of starting over and losing any progress I had made along the way.

As I grew older, I started facing these challenges head-on and, one by one, started to conquer them like a knight who faces a menacing dragon. This resulted in many bruises and time lost healing from the wounds of battle. I believed that I only had these two choices: to slay the dragon or to run away. I have now adopted a third option: to ride the dragon, using its power to help me in my quest to become stronger than ever before.

We must remove the things in our lives that are not giving us the results we are seeking. I remember an intern working in the garden one day. She looked up, surrounded with the light of a beautiful epiphany, and she said, "We are pulling weeds in this garden to make room for the things we want to grow. This is the same work I am doing in my life. I am making room for the things I want to grow." We can learn so much in the garden.

Now I am grateful for feelings of heartache and do not try to avoid them. Now I face difficult challenges with grace because I see them as teachers who share a way of thinking without attachment to outcome. I anticipate greatness to occur all around me without the expectation of what that looks like. I have designed my life so that every morning is fueled from the fires of yesterday, creating a regenerative and abundant tomorrow.

Activity 5:
Create a Map of your Life

Have your functional analysis with you for this activity and the network list you created in chapter five.

- ❖ Start by drawing where you live in the center of a blank piece of paper. (Zone 0)
- ❖ Now add all of the activities from the functional analysis activity from chapter four on the map relative to where they occur in your life. Place things closer to your house closer to the middle and things you must travel farther away.
- ❖ Next add the relationships you identified from your network list that you created in the activity in chapter 5. Place each "match" on the map where the exchange takes place.
- ❖ Now draw a line from your house to each activity and then back again. You will create a loop for each trip you make for an activity. Try to see if you can include any of your relationships into these trips.
- ❖ Observe if any of these trips should be part of other ones. Notice how each of these things can be connected in more ways. Try to make as few loops from your house as possible but still connect all relationships and activities.

You should now have a list of needs, yields, things that make you strive as an individual, and where they are physically located in your life of abundance. Now it is time to start implementing a plan! Hopefully you are able to find connections and add more things into your life that you have identified as important to you and they will be fed by other equally important activities and relationships creating more abundance and happiness in your life.

CHAPTER 7

Relationships

"Realize that everything connects to everything else."

- Leonardo da Vinci

IF I HAD TO DEFINE PERMACULTURE using only one word, that word would be relationships. As we continue to build the bridge between our inner landscape and ecology in this text, you may start to realize that everything is delicately and precisely connected and lies somewhere on a spectrum between stress and harmony. When I am designing a Permaculture system, I try to create ecosystems with as little stress as possible by designing all components of the system to be connected to at least two other elements. For example, a rainwater catchment system will feed a hand washing sink and the waste water from the sink will drain into a wetland system growing taro or other edible aquatic plants. Each system supports the other systems creating breathtaking abundance. This way of thinking is different from a typical industrial linear system that creates waste and is focused on mass production and not regenerative sustainability.

One of the most repeated questions I'm asked in the garden is how to get rid of pests. I explain that a plant that grows in healthy soil with a strong soil web and microorganisms present will be resilient against pest infestation. A healthy plant will be able to fight off pests and disease just like a healthy body can fight off a cold. This answer is always immediately followed by "Yes, but what do I spray on the plants to kill the pests?" This is the problem with conventional thinking. We have accepted the belief that we can change and control everything in an ecosystem without any consequence of how our actions affect the delicate relationships that are in place. We believe we can spray poison to kill whatever is inconvenient, like weeds or insects; however, the truth is that this also kills the beneficial microorganisms in the soil. When they die the soil health declines and the organic matter in the soil degrades. The soil is then no longer suitable to host the microorganisms that produce nutrients for the plants. The plants become weak and unhealthy.

In the conventional food production system, you are urged to use chemical fertilizers to supply the nutrients that the microorganisms were supplying before the insecticide killed them. Now the delicate soil web is completely destroyed and the abundant natural relationship between the earth and the plant has been replaced with a toxic chemical one. Sir Albert Howard wrote *The Soil and Health* in 1957. This book explains the wonderful symbiotic relationship that exists between our health and that of the soil. When we can see the pests in our garden, not as a problem, but as an indicator of what we can do better, then we are on the path of living in abundance and harmony in nature.

Terence McKenna said, "Nature is not mute; it is man who is deaf." When I am doing a site assessment on a property, I will first look at the weeds that are growing there. I treasure these little storytellers where others may go to great lengths to get rid of them. I can tell if a property floods, has acidic or alkaline soil, and I can create a potential plant list simply by looking at the weeds that are present. I can get a snapshot of how nature places plants on the land without any human inputs. When I explore the existing relationship of plants and animals on the land, I can understand them better and then help to shape a system that will not require many inputs to maintain and will create an abundance of resources. Simply by being aware of the relationships that exist and respecting their delicate balance in the ecosystem we can integrate ourselves without creating toxic situations. As the apex species on the planet, we have the unique ability to put a beneficial handprint on the world around us. We can create six inches of compost in three months compared to the 2,000 years a forest would need to create the same amount simply by understanding how these intricate relationships in nature are interacting with each other.

This skill can also be discovered in social settings. There are many more humans on the planet than ever before in history and they all think very differently, resulting in many broken relationships. If we compare these to weeds in the garden, we can see come amazing similarities. If we have a closed mind, we only hear disagreements and criticism but, if we open our hearts to hearing other people's opinions, we can hear the love and support from our fellow humans. There is a sweet compassion discovered when listening to things you may not agree with. To let go of the idea of being right and listening with an open heart can be a very challenging task. My father and I did not agree on many things. Our views on the environment, politics and racial equality were all very different. This created a rift in our lives that was not healed until only weeks before his death. My father died of cancer and I was able to spend time caring for him in the tender days before he passed. When I saw him in his weakened state, I no longer had the energy to disagree with him or try to convince him that I was right about anything. I was able to see through our disagreements into a space of connection and our relationship grew exponentially in that time. I remember feeling regret that I had not let go of our disagreements sooner. This is when I first realized that it is more important how we make people feel than whether we are right or wrong. I wasted so much time trying to be right in my personal opinion that I missed spending precious, quality time with my father. I am learning to accept the opinions of others as sacred and treat the thoughts of others as I would my own because nothing is more important than standing in a place of love and understanding. The more we are all heard and understood, the more we will be able to share our passion and dreams with each other without fear of being attacked or ridiculed. To understand the value in everyone's opinions is similar to understanding the value of the weeds in your landscape.

Now is a perfect time to become responsible for our part in the relationship with our ecosystem. We tend to shift the burden of environmental destruction for our personal convenience and convince ourselves that we are not doing anything wrong. If we are to be in harmony with our planet and each other we must have integrity with our words and actions. How can we say we want a better world for our children in one breath and then support a toxic industrialized food system that is destroying the planet in the next? The two are intricately connected and when we become aware of this relationship, we can see that our actions or inactions are responsible for a part of the situation. We must be willing to take action to achieve the outcomes we support. Your thoughts will determine your actions and your actions will determine your future.

Communication plays such an important role in maintaining healthy relationships. As we become more socially disconnected from each other our communication skills are decreasing in quality and effectiveness.

Conversations can often echo divisive reflections of our thoughts. In a society based on separation, we are witnessing a decreased quality and authenticity in our relationships.

Nature is built on a system of reciprocity. An example of this can be seen in an old oak tree. The tree takes nutrients, water, and carbon dioxide from the earth and starts the miracle of growth. However, it does not hoard these things, but instead, it shares its leaves and decomposing matter to feed the systems under it. This cycle creates abundance and harmony. When we add human greed into the system, resources get taken out of circulation, which causes stagnation and decreases the health of the whole system. Indigenous tribes would treat this greed as a mental illness where as it is rewarded with wealth in today's society.

The Iroquois had a philosophy that the decisions we make today should result in a sustainable world seven generations into the future. Every decision we make should result in sustainable relationships for future generations. Just like the tree shares its nutrients with the forest all around, we could share our energy with our neighbors. The more that we separate ourselves from our ecosystem, we create relationships that are unhealthy and can even become toxic. We can see this manifest in the form of gossip within a community. Gossip can create division and affects quality of life for the whole community by creating confusion and doubt. The more connected we are in our relationships, the stronger we will be as individuals. One day as I walked into a store to buy a few things I witnessed the person in front of me in line texting as they were checking out. They handed the cashier money, accepted the change, and took their items all without saying a word or making eye contact with the cashier. I saw this as a warning sign of where our disconnected culture could be headed.

We have forgotten that our relationship to each other is just as valuable as any product or service. This is reflected in how we do not listen to the natural world around us as issues like climate change and water health become louder and louder. We are willingly walking into a world where we are separated from nature and from each other. It is becoming normal to look the other way. We check our phones before we say good morning to our loved ones and we are still using toxic chemicals to grow our food. We have become proficient at ignoring the signs of the failing relationships around us resulting in superficial and ineffective interactions with the earth and with our community.

I see social injustice and discrimination in our society as a direct reflection of our disconnection with nature. When we see humans as part of nature it is easy to understand the importance of social diversity and cultural openness and integration just as all diversity is an essential part of a healthy ecosystem. We can see how this disconnection with the natural world manifests around us as we examine how we isolate our culture the same way that we monocrop our food. These are both similarly tragic and destructive practices. When we isolate cultures, we create systems that are less resilient to irregular changes in the environment, such as natural disasters and even social upheaval. Great strength and stability come from a focused effort from many different sources. A single thread cannot bear much weight but, woven together, a blanket can lift a heavy load. I believe the first step in healing the relationships in social systems based on inequality is to acknowledge the privilege and power that the beneficiaries of these systems receive at the expense of others. This is easy to observe in systemic racism and oppression exhibited around the world. This inclusionary truth must be openly and honestly examined. There must be a clear agreement that future systems must be strictly built with equality and respect for all life and to advances the entire system, not just a self-selected powerful few. I pray we can thrive together in a world of love and respect, built on a foundation of tolerance and equality.

Every relationship you will experience in your adult life starts as a reflection of the relationship you have with yourself. I have personally struggled with authentically feeling self-love. This has resulted in me looking outside of myself to feel complete. I have had feelings of not being good enough or smart enough and this challenged most of my personal interactions, resulting in codependent relationships in which I was trying to find love and validation through others. Now I remind myself to try to come from a place of integrity and self-love every day. I remind myself that it is ok if I'm not right all the time or if someone doesn't like me. I have, instead, promised myself to act from integrity and to live with an open heart without fear of being rejected. A daily practice of reminding myself of the things I love and the dreams I want to accomplish has helped me tremendously. We are all beautiful and powerful beings of love, light, and creation, capable of doing amazing things. The more we create a strong and healthy relationship with ourselves, the more we will see thriving relationships around us. Several years ago, I started to focus on my personal relationships and the quality of my interactions with others. I found that a mind that is pure will find purity in any situation whereas a clouded mind can pollute even the sweetest of relationships. I am now enjoying sharing relationships that are powerful, clear, and beautiful, absent of expectations and judgment. Seeing the best in people in my community has surrounded me with some of the most amazing people imaginable and as this positive energy surrounds me, it has attracted more positivity into my life.

I have seen a shift in human consciousness and awareness like I have never witnessed before. I see the next generation driven to stand up for social justice and heal our planet in rapidly increasing numbers. I spent some time trying to understand why this increase was occurring and I developed a theory. Pioneer species are hardy plants which are the first to colonize barren environments that have been disrupted, such as by fire or natural disasters. They start a chain of ecological succession, which results in a fertile, diverse, and stable ecosystem. I believe that the earth has been disturbed by toxic human culture that accepts destructive methods of food and energy production exacerbated by consumerism and exponential population growth. I predict that, as these young minds grow and influence the culture around them, a succession of earth-friendly humans will rise up and honor the relationship we share with this planet to help restore a healthy and regenerative future.

I have spent a large part of my life trying to motivate people to care about our environment and our relationships. As we heal the relationships with our planet, our communities, and ourselves we can invite the beautiful image that lives within our hearts to manifest around us to create a world of abundance. As we remove the obstacles of self-doubt, expectations, and ignorance we will have a clear projector to send our vision of a sublime world into a physical existence. This journey begins with us and can carry us into our wildest dreams. We are here to discover our passion and put that passion into action. We are here to make a difference in the world. We are the pioneer species for a regenerative future.

Activity 6:
Write a Personal Affirmation

Using an affirmation or statement said with confidence about how you want to see yourself during your day can have many positive effects. An example of an affirmation is "I am compassionate and I care how people feel." As you repeat the words to yourself, you will begin to subconsciously believe the statements. This will help you embody these qualities, which will affect how you interact with people around you and create new opportunities in your enhanced life of abundance. Write a personal affirmation that best describes how you want others to see you and how you want to see yourself.

- Start with the words "I am." This is because we are rewriting any old thought patterns.
- Stay in the present tense. This is because if we talk in the future, we are giving ourselves permission to wait for the result.
- Start with believable affirmations and work your way to bigger and better ones as you continue to practice.
- Keep the affirmations brief and specific to what you truly want.
- Repeat them as often as possible. Once, twice, three times a day... and every time one pops into your mind

It is very important to not just say them, but also really believe them. Envision yourself as the person who embodies these affirmations.

Affirmations can be a powerful tool to help you change your state of mind and manifest the change you desire in your life. Try repeating your new affirmation for the next seven days and see if you notice any difference in the way you feel. If you feel like it helps, add this practice into your daily routine.

CHAPTER 8

Wellness and Health

"A nation that destroys its soil destroys itself."

- Franklin D. Roosevelt

THERE ARE MANY COMPONENTS that make up a complete healthy and happy life. It is ultimately essential that we find a regenerative balance between nurturing the physical body, the emotional body, and supporting the health of the planet. In Permaculture, we are introduced to three ethics: care of the earth, care of the people, and fair share or resource distribution. We have discarded these ethics in our modern industrialized culture in exchange for higher profits that have left the ecosystem and us in an unhealthy state. In this chapter, we will explore the capacities of emotional and physical health and the importance of our global relationship to the ecosystem that is needed to maintain a healthy and thriving life of abundance.

We must all learn to support our emotional health in conjunction with maintaining the physical body. A dear friend who served in the United States Military was trained for years to take orders and not allow awareness to his emotions. He was trained not to think or feel. Shortly after his service he discovered that by ignoring his emotional body, his physical health began deteriorating. After this realization, he started to meditate daily and began a daily yoga practice giving him new insight into his emotional health. This balance between mental and physical health created a state of wellness he had not felt since he was a child. He now understands the truth that the physical and emotional bodies are deeply connected and that by living on only one side of the spectrum, he experienced a disharmonious existence and more physical ailments.

Our physical bodies are projections of the images we hold true in our emotional bodies. When we constantly ignore our emotions or keep ourselves in a state of anxiety, we can cause unintentional damage by projecting images of stress and disease to our physical bodies.

There are many ways to cultivate a tranquil and harmonious state of inner peace. My personal favorite is the five-thousand-year-old practice of yoga. Yoga began in India where it was personally handed down from guru to student. It uses physical postures, breath-work, and meditation as tools to master the mind, control the emotions, and grow spiritually. The practice was brought to America where its deep spiritual nature has been lost and physical fitness is emphasized. An important aspect in yoga is the use of meditation to develop mindfulness and clarity. During meditation, practitioners slow their thoughts to maintain a single point of focus. A word or mantra can help eliminate distractions and create stillness in the mind.

A good metaphor for the practice of meditation is the use of swales in Permaculture. The swale is a trench that is dug level on the land so that it will catch water as it flows down the slope of the landscape. This level trench keeps the water on the property, making it available for use by plants and animals within the system. In meditation, we stop the energy from rolling past us and, instead, we direct it and let it sink in so it is available for use within the entire internal system.

The practice of meditation can help create a state of mind in which we dissolve distraction and temptation, creating a stillness as beautiful and as peaceful as lying in a field of flowers on a sweet summer's day. If we do not cultivate this stillness, it is easy to get distracted by the "monkey mind"; jumping from tree to tree, aggravated by the busy world around us. This can lead to anxiety, stress, and depression. Many doctors prescribe antidepressants or other mood stabilizers due to these symptoms. I believe there are cases where psychotropic drugs are useful in patients with chemical imbalances and severe trauma, but I believe that the practice of using pharmaceutical drugs for mood stabilizing is similar to using insecticides in your garden. It is effective at getting rid of the pest, but it does not address the real issue and actually can make the situation worse in the future. When we mask our emotions with prescription drugs, we create a dependency and an artificial stability in our thoughts instead of learning to develop, experience, and appropriately respond to our feelings.

The practice of meditation has been providing a pathway to inner peace and mental clarity for thousands of years without the use of these medications. Modern science has recognized the beneficial effects meditation has on the brain and mental health.

Meditation and yoga are not the only avenues to a clear mind; part of the joy of this life is to find the one that resonates the most with you. My favorite part of this adventure is once you find a method of taming your thoughts, then it is time to put your thoughts into action. When we put a clear mind into action filled with passion, our lives begin to emanate purpose and meaning. This existence can easily manifest into a life full of health and wellness.

The best method to prevent disease is to have a healthy immune system. A weak or stressed system will invite disease and illness, much as pests will invade a weak or poorly nourished plant. The quality of our food determines the building blocks we use in building our strong and resilient immune system. In economically impoverished areas where fresh, nutritious food is harder to find, it is often one of the first things to be cut from home budgets. This can quickly materialize into mental fatigue and health issues due to poor diet.

I started growing my own food because I could not afford to buy organic food in the grocery store. I still remember my first harvest of cherry tomatoes. They were sweeter and juicier than any I have had from a store. I could feel the energy enter my body as I ate them. I knew at that point that being personally connected to the food we eat is a precious part of the human experience, even if it is only a mental awareness and appreciation.

Today, the average food item in an American grocery store travels 1000 miles before it gets to the shelf. It is harvested, packaged, and shipped with much less love and attention than your backyard veggies would receive. Commercially grown food is typically grown using pesticides, herbicides, and chemical fertilizers that are destructive to our ecosystem. The food is wrapped in plastic and shipped using petroleum-fueled vehicles; all these practices are toxic to our bodies and our planet.

Are you surprised that health problems have increased steadily since the introduction of an industrialized food system? Plants grown commercially are chosen based on ease of shipping and appearance, instead of nutrition. The wheat grown by indigenous cultures was 12 times more nutritious than conventional wheat grown today, but because it grows 16 times more slowly, it is not as profitable to grow this variety. Agribusiness trades nutrition for profits, resulting in illnesses.

There is a feeling that is hard to describe when we put our hands into fertile soil. I can feel the energy of the earth as I work the land. I look forward to my time in the garden harvesting and planting. It fills me with energy, hope, and inspiration. There's a feeling of great accomplishment when I have a wheelbarrow full of potatoes or a basket full of delicious organic greens. This positive energy I feel is then transferred into the food I eat.

As technology advances and the global economy grows, the amount of daily physical activity the average person engages in decreases, resulting in our species being less physically fit. A study in 2013 analyzed the health of 25 million children ages 9-17 from around the world. The results showed an increase of 90 seconds in the time required to run a mile. This is attributed to weight gain resulting from the introduction of televisions, computers, and sedentary lifestyles, along with the introduction of high fructose corn syrup into our diets. One of the many beneficial side effects of growing our own food is getting exercise while we are doing it. When we mix physical exercise with a diet of organic food, we have the basic recipe needed for maintaining a healthy body.

Imagine the earth as a singular living system with all the plants and animals connected. When we look at the earth through this lens, we see humans are also part of this larger organism, much like the cell is part of the human body. If we look at the illnesses affecting us today, we can see similar illnesses affecting the earth. The rivers are polluted with the same heavy metals that are in our blood. Land, sea, and air are filled with human-made pollutants that show up in our bodies. Our individual health is directly related to the health of the planet. We must consciously care for the environment, as we are part of it and it is part of us.

Health and wellness are affected by our ability to take care of our minds, bodies, and environment. We cannot take a single leg away from this trio and expect the whole thing to remain standing. They are all equally important. There are several tools available to us to find and maintain this balance. I invite you to integrate one or all of these into your lifestyle and experience the benefits.

1. Drink Water: Humans are more than 60 percent water, and our blood is about 90 percent water. Water is essential for the kidneys and other

bodily functions. It is a very good habit to drink a large glass of water when you wake up to provide your body with this life-giving resource. Water is needed in the processes of sweating, oxygenating the body, and waste removal. If the kidneys and bowels do not have enough water, waste can build up inside the body and cause problems. Dehydration affects the skin and how the brain functions. Without water, we may experience mental fatigue or have trouble focusing. Prolonged dehydration can result in headaches and illness. If you're sweating or doing strenuous exercise, make sure to increase your intake of water. Drink lots of water to keep your body hydrated.

2. Eat Healthy Food: Diet affects our mental and emotional health as well as the environment. I always recommend trying to grow your own food. Homegrown foods have more beneficial nutrients and contain fewer pesticides than conventional foods. Fungicides, herbicides, and insecticides are widely used in conventional agriculture and residues stay on what we eat. Fresh grown foods will not contain preservatives to make them last longer for shipping. If you are unable to grow your own food, try to get to know a farmer or organic food co-op. Eating healthy is a wonderful habit to adopt and will improve your mental, physical, and emotional health.

3. Do Affirmations: As we learned in the last chapter, an affirmation is the action of acknowledging something you want into existence. A daily affirmation practice can improve clarity and focus. You'll become aware of your daily thoughts, words, and feelings, thereby reducing the risk of letting negativity sneak in. Being more focused on your goals serves to encourage and motivate you. You may also realize an increase in self-confidence or self-esteem. By simply telling yourself you are capable of greatness, you may find it easier to start reflecting the affirmation in your actions.

4. Create Morning and Evening Routines: The certainty of a routine helps us manage the uncertainty that life can throw at us. Having a daily routine can reduce the stress and anxiety in our lives. It can help us to cultivate positive daily habits and organize things that are most important to us. Sleep is really important for our mental health, and going to bed and waking up at scheduled times puts the body in a healthy cycle. This predictability can reduce stress and provide a strong foundation on which you can build positive, productive days.

5. Make "To-Do" Lists: A to-do list is a great way to organize the things we want to do in a day. It creates a framework but also gives a strategy for how to accomplish goals. You can visualize all of the things you want to do and prioritize what is most important. It is nice to have this to-do list if you find yourself with a little free time. You can simply glance at the list and pick one task instead of having to think about what you need to do. It is a great feeling to cross items off your list; it gives you permission to relax. This will provide you with stress-free downtime in which you can be more present.

Once you write your list, you have given it power. Now that your list has power, don't habitually leave things undone. If you really can't finish them all, acknowledge that. Otherwise, undone tasks may pile up and contribute to anxiety.

6. Be Conscious and Authentic with Your Words: The more you speak with honesty and integrity the more you will be surrounded with positive and healthy relationships. You will have more confidence because you will know your words and actions come from a place of integrity. Your life will become more meaningful because your words, actions, and passions are all aligned. You will likely be more successful in business because people will

be able to trust you and opportunities will present themselves. People will want to include you in their projects.

7. Journal Daily: Journaling about things you love allows your brain to relive the moment and offers a chance to recreate the feelings. The awareness of doing what you love will boost your self-esteem. There is a connection between happiness and mindfulness. Journaling brings us into that state of mindfulness and self-awareness that helps us focus in the present moment. Journaling about your dreams and ambitions can provide an outlet for processing emotions. Journaling also provides something for you to reflect on as you grow through life. I always keep a daily journal when I travel. Whenever I feel like I am stagnant in life I just open up a journal from 15 years ago and relive the adventures I encountered. I remember the lessons I learned from each of them. Remember to be kind and patient with yourself in this new process. Try journaling first thing in the morning or before sleeping. You may find that this new routine becomes the favorite part of your day.

The most important part of the journaling process is getting the pencil to the paper (or the fingers on the keyboard). Just allow yourself to write whatever thoughts come to you. You can start with recalling conversations that made an impression on you or simply what you had for breakfast. It helps some people to treat the journal like an old friend you want to share your day with. It is important not to judge yourself or think too much about the content of what you write. It may not make sense to you in the moment, but it is not important to understand. The idea is to trust the process and give your creative mind an outlet to express the subtle thoughts that would otherwise go unheard. As I write this book, I often find myself in a trance-like state, typing for hours. When I review the pages I have written, it is like reading someone else's words. This strange phenomenon has made me think about where these thoughts come from. When we create the opportunity for our inner voice to speak, our bodies become a conduit for our wisdom to flow through. If we are truly attuned, our wisdom is aligned with the wisdom of the universe.

8. Positivity: Positivity is contagious. We are constantly affecting everyone around us. I remember moving into a rural neighborhood outside of Orlando, Florida, where the community did not interact much and everyone kept to themselves most of the time. I quickly made friends with the next-door neighbor and built a chicken coop where we shared the chore of feeding and caring for the birds, along with the egg harvest. I eventually started seeing chicken coops popping up all over the neighborhood and soon everyone had an abundance of farm-fresh free-range eggs. This quickly expanded to veggie gardens and potluck dinners, and eventually the neighborhood became a connected community, sharing surplus with each other.

Each of the practices described in this chapter has played a key role in helping me develop my personal health and wellness. By doing the work needed to get yourself into your best state of health possible, you can have the greatest positive impact on your community. I have found it easier to focus on the health of others and the health of the planet if I am physically and mentally healthy myself. Just like a lifeguard has to be physically healthy to save a drowning victim, we all must be healthy to help each other. In this way, we can create happy, healthy communities filled with happy, healthy humans.

Activity 7:
Create a Daily Activity Schedule

A daily schedule will help you structure your life and acquire a rhythm to your day. Just like the sun rises and sets on a schedule, we can benefit from creating a structure for our lives. I recommend starting your day with a practice of gratitude and affirmations to help frame the rest of your day so I have included this into the schedule. Now let's design your perfect day. Begin by asking yourself the following questions:

- When do I like to wake up?
- When do I like to work and when do I feel most productive?
- When do I like to dedicate time to learning or advancing my hobbies?
- When do I like to eat meals?
- How many hours of sleep do I need and when do I like to go to bed?
- Use the chart on the following page to fill in these structured parts of your day.

You may find that the answers to the questions do not match the life you are currently living. For example, if you feel most productive in the morning but you are currently working the overnight shift, you may want to look at ways you can work during your most productive hours. This is not only beneficial to you but for your employer as well. Use this schedule every day for the next 10 days. If you feel better and you are more productive, continue to use and fine-tune your new schedule.

Name:

Time of day	**Activity**	**Duration**	**Notes**
	Wake Up		
	Self-Care		
	Daily Practice	30 Minutes	Gratitude/Yoga/Affirmations
	Prepare for Sleep		
	Reflect on your Day		
	Plan for Tomorrow		
	Sleep		

CHAPTER 9

Service

"Love all, Serve all, Feed all"

- Neem Karoli Baba

WHEN I FIRST STARTED TRAVELING with the Rainbow Gathering Tribe, I didn't get extremely involved with the community at first. I was there to experience the hippie free love, counter culture, and spiritual community lifestyle they had to offer. During this time, I felt isolated and on my own journey. My days were filled with superficially gratifying experiences and did not have much meaning. Then I got involved with the Granola Funk Kitchen, a hip and health-conscious group of individuals dedicated to feeding people good food. I began washing dishes for the kitchen because I felt an internal need to give back to a community that fed me and taught me so much about living peacefully together. While washing dishes, I started to meet people and get involved in community activities. More opportunities were presented to me until, eventually, I started working at a space called "tea time" which is a space where tea is served and people listen to each other tell stories and interact in a community setting. This is the most connected I ever felt at the rainbow gatherings. My identity in the community resonated with how I wanted to live my life and it was the first time I can remember feeling like my words and actions were genuinely aligned.

A great sense of personal satisfaction can be felt when we put our love into action. Not only can we see the results of this action, but it also creates a vibration within us that resonates with why we imagine we are alive.

In Permaculture, engaging in a group action called a Perma-blitz plays an important role in the community. A Perma-blitz is a gathering of people who focus on an individual project to work on together. This is similar to the Amish community where everyone will come together and build a barn for a family in need. When many people come together, you can accomplish a miraculous amount of work in a very short time. This strengthens the individual and the group at the same time.

Society has been shifting into a culture of people wanting something in return for any action they take. I believe this is a result of the capitalist system that has been established and accepted as the "American dream". This economic system is good at motivating people but does not account for building community, especially communities with few monetary resources.

When my friend Kim reached out for help building a greenhouse on her farm, my first thought was, "How much are you going to pay me? What do I get out of this?" I was persuaded to help her without any monetary payment and we constructed a beautiful greenhouse where she grew plants for farms and families in the community to give away in order to create new gardens for people who wanted to grow food. I witnessed dozens of gardens created from the construction of this one greenhouse and ate at many potluck dinners with vegetables from those gardens. When we step out of an economic model and start to value community, experience, and relationships, this can start to change how we allocate our time and energy. When making money is the ultimate goal, it is not always advantageous to spend time helping your local community. I like to look at every business transaction as an opportunity to explore a new personal relationship. One of the biggest obstacles to this is big box stores and large corporations focused on profits. Large chains with low prices funnel business and money away from locally-owned stores and force them out of business, creating a community dependent on the big store, leaving less money in the local economy, and depleting local resources and relationships.

It is simple to say that these businesses utilizing unethical labor and environmentally destructive practices are causing the problems but we are the ones paying them to do it. We are willingly trading our stable local economy and environmental health for low prices. These businesses venture that you will choose their store over the local store to save a few bucks. What you may not see is the environmental destruction and social injustice that doing business on this scale creates. That is the hidden price behind the lower prices. The more independent and regenerative a community is, the fewer resources it requires from the outside world. We can help each other grow food locally by pooling our resources and working together. We can help each other create wealth in the form of regenerative energy and tool sharing creating less need for outside resources. There are two ways to get rich: make more or use less. When we support a system that profits on our inability to supply our own food, energy, and water we remain disconnected and dependent. This creates an illusion of dependance and helplessness. The truth is that we are all connected to the natural world in countless ways. Working together for the health of the planet and the growth of our local communities helps us all grow and thrive together. There is no quicker path to inclusion than to be in service to those immediately around you. As you start tending the garden of kindness, flowers of love and compassion will start to bloom all around you.

My father was a very isolated man. He did not have many friends and rarely participated in social or service-based activities. He once asked me how I was able to surround myself with so many friends and have such loving people around me. After reflecting on this question, I came to a realization: whatever you give out into the world is what the world will give back to you magnified. Gandhi spent many years teaching non-attachment to material possessions. Today, more than fifty years after his death, many statues I have seen of him have flowers and gifts at its base. I enjoy putting love and compassion into the world and to everybody I meet and I am constantly amazed as that love and compassion reflects back to me in ways I could never have imagined.

Let us explore four levels of actively practicing compassion:

1. True Compassion for Yourself: This includes being gentle with yourself and not beating yourself up for every past mistake. This takes some practice, as it is easy to identify with your past actions. You are not these actions and you can reinvent yourself at any time in any way you choose. To have compassion for yourself allows you to step away from your mistakes and rise above them.

2. **Compassion for Those That you Love:** This one is often easier for most people because you care for these people based on your relationship and history together and you genuinely want the best for them. This level can be challenging for selfish or egocentric individuals who find it difficult to care for things and people outside themselves.

3. Compassion for People you Don't Know: To care for people you do not know can be challenging because society generally teaches us to take care of our families and ourselves first. To understand that helping those around us is the same as helping ourselves can be a difficult concept to understand. This can include altruistic work like feeding the homeless and going out of your way for people you've never met before. This level of compassion can change a community by lifting each member up out of difficult situations and into a space of love and support.

4. Compassion for All that is Equal to Compassion for the Self: I have found this to be a challenging level of compassion. To care for all sentient life as if it were your own. I have witnessed beautiful people act with great urgency, as if it were affecting their immediate personal health in environmental rallies and demonstrations around the world. This level of compassion could change the world if everyone practiced it. The way we do business and interact with each other would change drastically if we cared for everyone in this way. Problems like starvation, homelessness, and mental disorders could all be significantly reduced and the world would be a better place for so many people.

One way to put your passion into action is by actively protesting the things you would like to change. Protests have been responsible for historically significant social change. Protest can include marches, demonstrations, collecting signatures, and public assembly. When a community collectively resonates on an issue, the volume is amplified and it is harder for people to ignore the message. It is important when we witness social injustice to express our intentions for a peaceful and healthy world for all.

One of the dangers of protesting is that your inner peace can be lost to the anger and frustration that initially motivated you to protest. When you focus on this anger it can become a debilitating part of your reality. Your conversations may become angry and your relationships may become based in conflict. This can begin to manifest into a very frustrating and intense lifestyle. I have seen very peaceful people become angry and depressed as they let the internal beauty of this world become overshadowed with human caused tragedy. This is very common in career law enforcement officers. After many decades watching people do horrible things, it is easy to only see things in this light. As much as I appreciate protest and I realize the power for social change, I recommend people remain in a state of love and kindness when you engage in the action. I believe that a protest based on anger and frustration rather than love and justice will magnify these negative feelings even if the protest is successful. Instead, I like to be the example of a human life filled with love and show people how kindness can permeate through society to make a change.

These examples will motivate people by demonstrating how positivity can make lasting change in local communities. When people experience a community filled with love and kindness, they will not tolerate a disconnected society rooted in anger and frustration.

We can all make a difference in changing and improving the lives of others and put the unity back in community. Volunteering has many wonderful benefits for you and the people you choose to serve. Find a cause that fills you with joy. Most neighborhoods have people or families in need, from elderly or handicapped shut-ins to struggling single-parent households. Reach out and find where you can be of the greatest service. Perform an act of random kindness and raise the vibration of your community. Bring flowers to your friends or the teachers at your child's school. Pay the tolls for several people behind you. You will see that people will pay this kindness forward. When I was in high school, I used to travel to other schools and be a mentor for troubled youth. Many organizations that work with troubled children need adults to be positive influences. By giving people an example of love and kindness, you give them a role model to emulate and goals to achieve. You cannot find that which you do not know exists.

One of my favorite acts of service is feeding the hungry. Hunger is a feeling that connects us all. Everyone reading this book has been hungry and had someone feed you. This fills not only our bellies but fills our hearts with gratitude so we can keep going in life. You can provide food for people you know or volunteer at a local soup kitchen or food bank. There is no greater gift than helping feed those in your community who are down on their luck and would go hungry if not for the service provided to them. If you are inspired to help our precious animals of the planet there are many animal shelters, rescue groups, or the humane society that constantly need help. Often times these organizations are run completely on volunteer support and really appreciate any help they receive.

I like to organize regular cleanups at local beaches and parks. This is a great way to get like-minded people together and remove garbage from the environment at the same time. You can pick up trash along the road, at a local park, or along the banks of a river. There are so many ways to give to your community and each of them will give back to you in more ways than you could ever imagine.

I moved to Hawaii in 2005 and gave away all of my possessions except for two duffel bags. As I began my new life on the islands, I started volunteering at local community gardens. I love working in the gardens and found one that appreciated the help. This work assisted me in meeting a community of like-minded people who loved the earth and wanted to make a difference. I developed deep friendships and new opportunities started to manifest. I was invited to a weekly local potluck dinner where we would harvest from the garden and make a delicious farm-to-table meal to share. Soon I was introduced to more local leaders and was asked to teach at a local school teaching environmental skills. My network of friends kept growing until one day I received a call from one of my musical heroes, Jack Johnson, asking for help in making a rain barrel. Jack has been in the environmental movement for years and is a leader in organizing eco-friendly benefit concerts and has always been a strong voice for positive change on our planet. I never would have imagined that I would be teaching an environmental superstar how to build a rain barrel. I went to his house the next week, met his family, and we built one of the most amazing rain barrels ever, and we painted it with flowers and rainbows. This relationship grew and I began working with the Kokua Hawaii Foundation. This amazing organization is a non-profit run by his wife, Kim

Johnson. I helped them build gardens for schools on the island of Oahu. Later that same year I initiated the installation of a regenerative solar energy system on Jack's home recording studio, Brushfire Studios. I went from not knowing anyone on the island on the other side of the world to hanging out with one of my favorite musical inspirations in less than two years. All of this love, opportunity, and friendship came from simply volunteering my time at a local community garden.

I think back to those days and it fills my heart with joy. I do not live in Hawaii anymore and I no longer share in those potluck meals or teach in those classes but I believe that part of me is still there. By offering my energy to a local community garden, I was rewarded beyond my imagination. There is no better way to meet people, develop new skills, open new opportunities, and fill your heart with gratitude than helping others grow and thrive. The quickest way to heal an ecosystem is to close the loop and connect to it. Helping people makes that community stronger and healthier-- and makes you stronger and healthier at the same time.

Activity 8:
Find an organization to help

Volunteering allows us to serve others and value things outside of ourselves. This activity will start you on an adventure of volunteering with an organization that reflects your personal goals. Follow the steps below to begin the journey.

- List 5 of your favorite community organizations in your area. Pick organizations with a mission that reflects your personal goals.
- Contact them by e-mail or phone and ask for volunteer opportunities and write down all the opportunities available and the time requirements for each.
- Determine which opportunities fit into your schedule and remove any that conflict with your current life.
- Review the available volunteer positions and organize them in the order of most interest to you.
- Call the first organization on the list and set-up your volunteer position.

Once you find a position you really enjoy, write down why you like the position. This will help you clarify what it is that you are seeking and what service fulfills you the most. There are many advantages to volunteering. Because you are not getting paid, there is more freedom to truly express your passion and provide a service to your community. Feel free to continue this volunteer position for as long as you feel it is rewarding or move to the next one on your list until you feel connected. Allow yourself to find new opportunities and relationships with your new position. As we help and heal others, we heal ourselves.

CHAPTER 10

Growth

"Life is a journey, not a destination."

- Ralph Waldo Emerson

EVERYTHING IN THE UNIVERSE is connected, and this synergy is fundamental for new growth to occur. It is often difficult to see because we are so close to all the complex relationships. If you stand too close to some Salvador Dali paintings, you cannot make out the image, so you must step back in order to see the whole picture. All of humanity is so tiny in comparison to the universe that our place in the equation is infinitesimal--and yet each of us affects the whole! Humans are just a small part of one ecosystem, and it takes many ecosystems interacting together to create a landscape, and many landscapes come together to create an environment, and this mosaic keeps stacking together until we construct the entire universe. The scale is so large we could never imagine making changes to the universe as a whole, but we can see our effect in our immediate ecosystem.

There are two types of ecosystems I want to discuss: natural and cultivated. In a natural ecosystem everything remains in balance. This natural homeostasis is what you would find in an undisturbed forest or ocean. In a cultivated system it has proven to be a little trickier to find that perfect state of relationship.

We have tried to recreate this balance in man-made closed-loop systems, such as a project named "Biosphere-2" in Oracle, Arizona. Complete with wilderness areas, a farm, and a small team of humans, this project was designed to work with as few outside inputs as possible. A privately funded venture, Biosphere-2 had the goals of providing education and ecotechnology development while testing the eco-laboratory they developed. The wilderness included a rainforest with a 25-foot waterfall, a grassy treed savannah, a desert, fresh and saltwater wetlands with mangrove trees, and a coral reef in a 25-foot-deep 150-foot-long ocean. A total of 3,000 species of plants and animals coexisted in Biosphere-2. The project managed to complete its two-year mission with only one emergency incident where they had to pump additional oxygen into the dome. The project eventually failed due to social collapse.

The closed-loop systems are used in space travel as well to create an environment that supports human life. NASA replicated the earth's atmosphere in the Apollo 12 for its return to Earth. Although cultivated ecosystems can function for brief periods of time, none have proven to be as effective or stable as a natural, closed-loop system. Nature has had millions of years to evolve and respond to change. It has grown from innumerable experiments through evolution. Humans have been unable to imitate the homeostasis of Earth's biosphere. I see humanity shifting into a time of growing awareness, and I believe each of us can play a role in creating new regenerative ecosystems.

Each one of us can make great change in the world. I was in a library in Australia when I saw an entire shelf dedicated to exchanging seeds in the community. I went to the desk and asked about this program and learned that a local woman had the dream of seeing more gardens in her community. She collected seeds, packaged them, and created the display. Her dream had grown into a program supported by hundreds. When I see this kind of action, I realize that each of us has the ability to make a significant difference in the world. Each of us can initiate this growth.

Have you ever been amazed when you see a seed sprout? Have you ever thought about the journey these seeds must endure before they become full-grown plants? Some pine tree seeds need to be burned by a brushfire before they will sprout, and the hard seeds of some native blackberries need to pass through the digestive system of an animal before they will germinate. Each of those seeds has the potential to become something great. If we imagine ourselves as those seeds and imagine all the challenges we have gone through as the requirements to sprout, we can more deeply appreciate the lessons needed to grow.

Most likely, growth will plateau if not built on a regenerative foundation. A wonderful example of this is modern economics. Our current economic system is built on the foundation of extracting natural resources and transforming them into financial capital. This system will grow as long as there are natural resources to extract. Unfortunately, resources such as oil, water, and fertile soil are being depleted quickly, which creates a toxic and depleted environment. In order to have sustained growth, we must turn the consumerist economic model into a regenerative one that more closely imitates the patterns of nature. Nature is built on the foundation of cycling nutrients through the entire system. As the nutrients are cycled, all parts of the system become healthy if they are productive or they adapt. If our economic system were imitating the patterns of nature, perhaps we would not be solely focused on financial gains but on other forms of capital available.

Ethan Roland wrote an amazing article on the eight forms of capital, in which he introduced new ways we can quantify value in different parts of our lives.

8 Forms of Capital:

- **Intellectual capital** - the things we know
- **Spiritual capital** - our personal practice
- **Social capital** - our friends and connections
- **Material capital** - things like buildings and tools
- **Financial capital** - the amount of money we have
- **Living capital** - things like trees or livestock
- **Cultural capital** - skills within a community
- **Experiential capital** - the things we see and do

Roland's work complements the work of Charles Eisenstein. With these new concepts I began to more deeply value the experiences I had. Once I broadened the scope of how I measured wealth, I began to value how my life was more diverse and enriched than when I was primarily focused on acquiring money. Until we can value all forms of capital, we will continue to create systems that deplete the health of our environment and have toxic relationships with our planet. Once we recognize what wealth really means to us, we can choose a direction for personal growth that better results in true abundance.

A consumerist society uses competition as the framework. People compete for jobs, money, and even parking spaces. Nature thrives when the system is built with cooperation as the foundation of growth. Trees will not hoard the leaves they drop, instead they will cycle the nutrients through the entire eco-system. This allows the entire system to grow and respond to disturbance and change together. Remember that the system will always change and react to environmental stimulus, so be prepared to accept the feedback you receive. Be open to respond to changes around you to help keep the whole system functioning most efficiently.

When designing our lives for health and abundance, we can start with a very simple foundation. The more we add material possessions and complexity to our lives, the more challenging it can be to find peace. When we are allured into materialism, we fall into a hidden trap of having to maintain the objects we have obtained, often adding complexity to our lives. They can become a financial burden and ironically take us further from abundance. I am not saying that we should not own anything or we should give away all of our possessions. I am suggesting that we take a close look at the things we choose to surround ourselves with and make sure that each item adds value to our lives. The more we shed the material possessions that do not support personal growth, the faster we will grow toward our true passion and achieve our goals.

When I do a property assessment for a new project, I start a conversation with the land during my initial barefoot walk through the site. With every step I am feeling the earth and asking questions. I feel the difference between the sunny spots and the shady areas. I notice the different plants that grow in each space. I observe the slope of the land and where water moves through the property. I let the land tell me where to put new elements into the system. I simply listen and respect what the land has to say. If there is a buggy area with poison ivy growing, I understand that these are important parts of the ecosystem.

Often designers come into an ecosystem and destroy the parts that are non-preferred. They will add new systems that they think are important, sometimes extinguishing the ecosystem that was previously there. However, those areas may have supported many species of plants and animals. It is our responsibility to value all life that is present and to understand that it has a purpose in the big picture. Making small and slow changes is a safe way to gently help shape the space while protecting and respecting the life present upon our arrival.

It is important to remember that we are all on our own individual journey. Perhaps you do not want to learn how to create a regenerative homestead with all of your food, energy, and water systems connected in a supportive and engaging community. There is absolutely no shame if your passion is to pursue the highest video game score or binge watching your favorite show. Our job is to find the garden that makes our hearts blossom. Just like every plant has the right place, every person has a setting in which they grow best.

When I catch myself judging others for doing things I do not appreciate, I try to remind myself that even though I may not personally prefer them, I recognize they have value and a place and purpose in the ecosystem. Even a destructive hurricane can have regenerative effects on the eco-system. The only difference in the beauty of a flower and a weed is in the judgment. I want to appreciate and accept everyone exactly as they are and without expectations of their actions or trying to change their minds.

It can be difficult to see the purpose of things we do not agree with. It has been a wonderful exercise for me to use compassion to understand why people do the things they do. Why is there war? Why are we killing the Earth? It is hard to find a purpose in these tragedies. This purpose could simply be to teach us as a species what not to do or they could be part of a larger story we do not understand yet. Finding a way to express our beliefs without filling ourselves with anger and resentment will often result in a more peaceful personal state of mind. This is not to justify any of the many egregious actions in the world, instead this is a way of nurturing our own inner peace so we can better express our thoughts and ideas to help humanity heal the wounds and better serve one another.

We cannot control how other people act or what they believe, but we can influence them by focusing on our own state of mind and actions. Think back to your last argument with someone. Now try to trace it back to the source of that argument. I have found most disagreements with others come from my expectations of their behavior. Often, they did not do what I wanted them to do or they disagree with my point of view. This expectation caused a suffering in me that manifested as fighting or turning them away. If we truly accept people for who they are and we do not place our expectations on their actions, the suffering attached to those expectations is able to transform into love and patience. There is a freedom that comes with letting go of expectations of how others should act. When we come from this place of acceptance, we experience personal growth and provide the space for others to grow as well.

It is also very important to surround ourselves with people who support the lifestyles we want. These people will influence the activities we do and the conversations we have. I sincerely enjoy being in the presence of like-minded people who truly appreciate and support my dreams and passions. The conversations I have with my friends empower me to create the life I dream is possible. They lift me up when I am weak and are a constant source of inspiration. These conversations feel deep and open my heart. This fertile ground is a perfect space for sprouting new ideas and healthy relationships that create abundance in multiple facets of my life.

A rich and full life is as achievable as an empty and meaningless one. There is a simple choice we are given to focus on the beauty of this world or not. I know we are all born into very different circumstances, but it is not important how easy things may seem for others, but instead, how we face our own challenges. I have seen many people lost in the trap of comparing themselves to others and experiencing bitterness and envy. There is little reward in this. We can choose to use our personal situation as an excuse for inaction. It is very common for people to want wealth and success but less common to be willing to do the work required.

It can take hard work to make changes in our lives. We make choices every day that will affect our situation. I really enjoy the sunrise, but it has been difficult to wake up so early. I started to set an alarm to wake up, and each day I would set the alarm 10 minutes earlier until eventually I would wake up before the sun welcome the sunrise. After doing this practice for several months, I started naturally waking up early without an alarm. Now the sunrise has become the favorite part of my day and I am grateful that I was willing to put in the work to add this beauty to my life.

As we stop giving power to our excuses, we can grow into a life that supports our passion. For most this starts with the job we choose. I believe we miss a great opportunity when we do not choose a job that supports our life's passion. When we trade our time for money doing things that do not really matter to us, we can create an attitude in which we are only willing to do the minimum of what is expected. When we have true passion for what we do, it is easier to be enthusiastic about every task. When I am working in the garden and I see people who show up early with excitement in their eyes, it gives me excitement and we become more productive together, which is contagious, and soon the entire garden is charged with this excitement and it becomes a place of more growth.

Education can be a powerful tool. However, it can also be a distraction. We are born with an empty and pure consciousness. This is why newborn children are surrounded in peace and innocence. They have not been taught greed, jealousy, or how to lie. The emptiness they experience gives them a simple peace that fades as they gain knowledge in life. We replace innocence with experience and slowly lose the perfect peace given to us at birth. Ironically, both education and emptiness are required for holistic growth. Seeking this balance has become a common practice in my day.

Many indigenous tribes have been exploring this balance for thousands of years, as can be seen in their ceremonies and rituals. As humans learn to balance respect for our Earth and integrate new technology, we will be on a new path for regenerative and sustainable growth.

When we can remember how to walk humbly on the earth as an integrated part of nature, we can once again join her in all of her abundance. To make that decision requires people who are willing to walk away from levels of comfort to which they have become accustomed. Many of these comforts are responsible for the destruction of this delicate balance with our eco-system. It does not make sense to grow in a direction that destroys the very foundation of life. Perhaps we will drive less or not be able to eat mangoes in February. I believe that sacrificing levels of familiar, modern comfort and convenience for the health of our environment is one of simplest and most effective methods of activism. These sacrifices are difficult and can take a long time to achieve. Remember that a rain barrel can take many drops of water to fill, but if you keep putting water in every day and keep focused, eventually you will achieve your goal. The lessons that are most uncomfortable are usually the most important, often with the greatest rewards.

There has never been a more urgent time to consider how the future growth of humanity will unfold and decide what our future will look like. We are responsible for the environmental destruction on this planet. We have created a situation in which we must re-learn to walk peacefully again. If we allow ourselves to accept this challenge and learn from our many mistakes, I believe we can create a life of abundance that is not based on ignorance, destruction, and greed.

I have never met anyone who has not felt pain and suffering. That leads me to believe that we are here to transform that pain into our own personal growth. Once we are able to navigate this transformation, it becomes our responsibility to help others do the same. Such evolution and growth can lead to a healthier and happier life for all.

Activity 9:
Make a timeline of your life

It can be very helpful to write down the adventures you have experienced in your life. The more we understand them, the more we can better understand how to shape our paths. Get a blank piece of paper and drawing supplies. It is not important to be a skilled artist, as long as you recognize what you are drawing later.

- Start in the center of the page and draw the place you were born.
- Next draw your childhood. Remember to add any relationships that influenced your life or stand out in any way.
- Continue with your drawing, moving on to the next influential life event creating the timeline of your life.
- You are finished when your drawing catches up with this current moment and all the most important moments of your life are on the page. Take a moment and really observe your drawing.
- After you have completed drawing your life timeline, write an entry in your journal with a narrative describing the entire journey in chronological order.

You are not defined by this timeline. This is simply a collection of events from your past. Each day we get to choose our actions and define our character. We can use past experiences as a foundation and a reminder to help guide us on our path to health and happiness. I sometimes recommend that people burn the picture they have drawn in a ceremonial fire as a way of letting go of any negative patterns you may have found yourself repeating. Sometimes these patterns are easy to see when we look at our lives in a linear drawing. Letting the picture burn can be a symbolic gesture to yourself that you are ready to move on and become the person you were born to become.

Chapter 11

Community

"If you want to go fast, go alone. If you want to go far, go together."

- African Proverb

YOU WERE BORN into a shared social arrangement that has been in motion for a very long time. This system most likely included components of fear and scarcity, designed to limit people from challenging the current social governing system. This ideology was present in most of the classrooms where you learned, commercials that you watched, and social gatherings you attended. Fear and isolation get people to believe they are separate from each other, producing a more manageable society with less revolt. You can see an example of this dating back to 400 B.C. when Socrates was executed for teaching the youth of Athens to think freely and question the church and government. When we learn to live closely with other open-minded people, the belief system strategically taught to us can be challenged and we get the opportunity to change our perspective and explore aspects of ourselves that often remain hidden.

Our personal weaknesses can be easily identified when reflected by those we trust and care for. I think of living together as putting rocks in a tumbler. They all grind against each other and erode the rough spots until each is a smoother version of itself. When we isolate ourselves, we do not have to identify these rough edges. We can convince ourselves there is no problem and that almost anything is normal. When we live alone, we are able to accept any truth we choose to believe and successfully hide the parts of our personalities that we choose not to acknowledge. Just as we cannot see our own faces without a mirror, we benefit from a community that will be honest and willing to kindly communicate the areas of our personalities that could improve, so we may grow and develop into our best selves. This process can be uncomfortable and painful.

I try to be an example of an enlightened human but I have been controlling, selfish, unkind, and disrespectful. It would be easy to hide these personality faults if I never had a community I loved to reflect them back to me. This brought awareness of the growth in which I could practice. I have learned to listen to my community and now want a circle of friends that objectively see my faults and inspire me to be a better person.

Learning how to communicate effectively is perhaps the most important skill you can practice to be successful in community. We must be able to express thoughts and ideas during times of conflict without holding onto negative emotions such as resentment or jealousy. This can require a great amount of practice and can be a very difficult skill to acquire. It can be equally challenging to listen to points of view with which you disagree.

I now try to listen to these ideas while keeping deep respect for the person sharing them. I remind myself not to become judgmental or defensive in my response. By sharing different points of view, we get the opportunity to see things differently and learn new things, and if after the conversation we still do not agree, I remind myself that we are all individuals who have the right to believe as we choose. From this place of love and respect we can continue the conversation without resentment and negative feelings. How we make each other feel can sometimes be more important than who is right or who is wrong.

I recommend creating a time when everyone in the community may share their thoughts and feelings in a safe and nonjudgmental space. I use sharing circles to achieve this goal. We sit so we can all see each other and take turns expressing what is important to us in that moment. I like to use a "talking stick" to keep things more organized such as a feather, a crystal, or a seashell. The object should have some meaning to the community and the item should be respected at all times during the session. The person holding the item is the only one in the circle who is allowed to speak. No one is allowed to interrupt or express any disagreements at this time. By creating a space for people to share what's in their hearts, a deep level of communication occurs that might never have had the opportunity to surface. This brings to light thoughts and feelings that can be addressed. You can include a time in the meeting to interact with each other and work together to solve any problems that may have been identified in the circle. If you are able to communicate kindly and effectively, it will be easier to solve problems and help each other grow.

Living in an intentional community is much more than simply living next to other people. It is easy to see the many differences between an apartment building and an intentional community. One of the benefits of an intentional community is the expression of interdependence. Interdependence can be defined as different parts of a system coming together to meet the requirements of the whole. One person in a group may love growing food while another is a skilled carpenter. Trading skills creates an opportunity for developing new connections. This relationship can produce a positive social interaction and result in less work for each individual, which creates a better quality of life for everyone.

I have seen many people in the world of Permaculture, especially those in the prepper movement, strive for complete personal independence.

They want to "make" their own food, water, and energy without being reliant on any outside inputs from others, including government or corporations, becoming completely sovereign. Whether this philosophy of independent isolation comes from political ideals or a premonition of a dystopian future, I do not personally subscribe to it. I believe that complete independence may create extreme separation and the loss of many advantages that being in community can provide. I believe in integration, not separation. As interdependence within the community increases, diversity and resiliency do as well.

Extrinsic characteristics are elements that appear because other elements are present. For example, a bicycle only works when there are tires, pedals, and a person riding. This creates a system that is more than the sum of all of its parts. The bicycle only works when all the parts are working together. When you create a functioning system, it feeds other systems and is fed by others. I am reminded of the story of a person's hand that goes on strike because it feels it's doing all the work feeding the body. So, the hand stops feeding the body and soon the whole person weakens and dies, including the hand! We all need each other in this world, and we all have different roles to play. This creates a beautiful cycle of abundance. In this interdependent model everyone is more connected and dependent on each other for both physical and social needs.

Interdependence of people can be compared to the practice of mulching in a garden. We mulch the plants in our garden for several reasons that compound on each other.

- ❖ A two-inch layer of mulch will prevent water from evaporating, keeping your plants hydrated.
- ❖ Mulch will also create a safe environment for bugs and microorganisms to live, and protect them from the elements.

These microorganisms will introduce nutrients to the soil as they procreate and die.

- The layer of mulch will reduce the space available for weeds to grow creating a garden that requires less maintenance.
- As the mulch breaks down, it adds valuable organic matter to the soil. This organic matter is essential for retaining nutrients and moisture in the garden.
- Finally, the addition of mulch has a pleasing aesthetic. It is often easier to feel at peace in a garden that is well-maintained and tidy.

Just by adding mulch, we see long-lasting regenerative effects on the garden as a complex system. Now imagine all the people in a town as the plants and the addition of shared community resources as the mulch which protects them and supports their growth. Simply by adding the element of sharing resources and experiences, they receive the many benefits of learning and growing together.

Social Permaculture explores interdependence in more detail. The Permaculture design principle, *integrate rather than segregate*, perfectly demonstrates this. As we combine systems, we build their resilience and increase their productivity. An example of this is a food forest where fruit trees outgrow trees planted in fields by themselves. By having a large variety of plants, we confuse pests and attract pollinators. The extrinsic characteristics of the food forest produce a fertile ground by supporting the community of microorganisms, helping each individual plant grow more vigorously. The healthier tree creates more shade and biomass to add to the entire system, creating a more abundant ecosystem rich in fertility and biodiversity.

This same concept applies to human communities. For instance, the more artists, dancers, and musicians that are in a community, the more fun and diverse events there are to attend. This creates a social abundance and a feeling of prosperity and connection. It is important in a thriving community to have diversity. A village with farmers and no carpenters is less resilient. We can design our communities in the same way we design our food forest. We can identify the niches that need to be filled and build social systems that feed and support those niches.

To further explore the effects of diversity, we look once more at the difference between a food forest and an orchard. By focusing on growing multiple types of trees, we increase the biodiversity which naturally occurs as more species are introduced. We want tall trees for the apex (top) layer followed by different size trees to fill all the space below. Different trees will grow roots at different depths. Therefore, we want to select plants that fill different niches of the soil horizon so the plants do not compete with each other. When a forest system is not overly competing, there is an abundance of growth and the whole system thrives. Similarly, in economics, when focused on a single source of capital, we lose the advantages of diversity. As we better understand our needs as individuals, we are able to see how we can best fit into our ecosystem without creating unnecessary stress and competition. By comparing social systems and economic systems to successful forest systems, we realize the many advantages of diversity and interconnection.

I have visited many intentional communities in several different countries in the past 20 years. They range in age from newly formed communities less than a year old to a village in New Zealand still thriving after 50 years. They all face different challenges and they all feel a little different, but they all share the awareness that life is easier and richer when we make the choice of consciously living together. We grow stronger when we actively lift everyone around us up and truly care for each other. I want to share with you some of the practices that impressed me the most in the intentional communities I have explored.

Tools for a dynamic community:

Resource sharing. In a cooperative model, resources are pooled together and shared. This happens in many ways, ranging from personal transportation to childcare to tools. When we do not duplicate possessions like automobiles and lawnmowers, this instantly creates wealth. As we design our homes and yards to require less maintenance, paired with sharing the tools needed, the community enjoys the benefits.

There are several ways to start this process. We can design much of the lawn space into edible gardens, creating food in these areas. The areas that are left for grass can be used for group picnics or gathering spaces and can be maintained by a collective. This means you only need one community lawnmower. This saves money and reduces requirements for maintenance and storage space. The surplus money can benefit the community as needed.

Sharing meal preparation is another great example of how working together can add efficiency and abundance. Imagine you live with 30 people in an intentional community. By creating a schedule, you can organize a system in which you cook one dinner a month for everyone, leaving about 29 days when the others prepare the meal. This not only reduces the number of days you need to make dinner, but also increases the diversity and variety of food you eat. This model also adds a lot of extra time for you to develop and realize your passions. As you use this newly acquired time to do more of the things you love, you are enriching the lives of the people around you, creating even more abundance.

Financial resource sharing. Where a conventional bank will give a loan, collect all the earned interest, and then send it off to a distant corporate entity, a savings pool is a locally held loan in which the earned interest returns to the pool for someone else to borrow. This model has numerous advantages for the local economy. The majority of the borrowed money remains local, and the projects that it funds often increases social and physical infrastructure. This type of private financing provides the opportunity to support each other and nurture local financial abundance.

There are many benefits of shopping and spending your money at locally aligned businesses. Not only are you building relationships, but you are also providing the local people with the financial capital they need in order to thrive. When I travel to a new town, I enjoy going to the local farmers' markets or family-owned shops. There you can meet local artisans and talk with people presenting the products they love to create. Typically, these conversations are far more exciting and informative than those I've had in chain stores. I instantly get a feel for the local energy and experience a connection to the people in the community.

Taking care of everyone as they age. I have witnessed people retire from lives where they dedicated the majority of their lives acquiring financial wealth, and I knew it was not the path I wanted. Even though I appreciate the value and privilege of financial stability, I believe that a community including family and friends surrounded with good food and engaging activity is far more valuable. For this reason, I like to invest my time and energy into my community as a plan for retirement and not just contribute to a 401K. As I envision myself older and unable to do the physical work of planting trees or maintaining fences, I want to take comfort knowing that the trees I planted many years ago are bearing fruit and that the next generation will be able to maintain what I have built and continue to build into the future.

Pooling human capital and gathering together. This is seen in Amish or Quaker establishments. I visited a Quaker establishment while in Australia and was impressed with their ability to consistently do this. I watched as they met in one large room, sat in a circle, and took turns sharing stories. They enjoyed a large meal they prepared together, shared the projects they were working on, and described what help they needed. It was here that I understood more deeply that we are stronger together.

The Amish will gather everyone together for a weekend and perform a barn raising where everyone helps build something for a family in the establishment. As this work helps one family, it also increases the quality of life for everyone by creating more abundance, prosperity, and a mutually supported sense of community. By seeing these examples, I began to appreciate how society can thrive in small, decentralized communities.

Is there is a limit to the number of social relationships an individual can successfully maintain? An answer was introduced in 1990 by a British anthropologist Robin Dunbar who proposed that humans could comfortably maintain approximately 150 or fewer stable relationships. Dunbar stated that larger numbers generally require more restrictive rules and laws to maintain stable social interactions. This creates disconnection within the community and can result in crime or other activities that can possibly lessen the quality of life for everyone. This number supports my understanding that smaller, more connected communities will be stronger and more abundant.

As much as I would love to tell you that living in community is the answer to all our problems and a simple way to create a life of happiness and abundance, I must express the challenges of choosing this lifestyle. The most difficult hurdle I have had to overcome is transitioning from an egocentric lifestyle. It has been hard for me to consider the welfare of others as a part of my own well-being. I have come to understand that the more individuals see the interconnected relationships with each other, the more the community will thrive as a whole. As an individual is lifted up within a group, the entire group is lifted up as a result of their success.

Another challenge is learning to have respect and consideration for others in situations that are not personally important. By not learning this skill, you can create unnecessary pain and suffering for the people around you. I remember an instance when a fence needed to be fixed in the community garden. Without talking to the person who maintained the garden, I went to work. I felt delighted to help in the task and completed the work in only two hours. Unknown to me, they had been planning a group activity to work on the fence for weeks and I had taken away their project. Ironically, I created stress and pain for them by fixing the fence. It has been a great practice for me to exercise awareness and vigilance in how others feel and how my actions will affect them. I now believe that people's feelings are often more important than getting the fence fixed.

I had a life-changing experience one day sitting on a composting toilet. I was feeling full of satisfaction knowing that I was not wasting drinking water or adding to a waste treatment plant with my offerings. I visualized how the chemicals that are used in the waste treatment plants eventually end up in local streams, rivers, and oceans and how they are not present in my beautiful regenerative privy. I was feeling like I was making a difference. I then started to compare this system of waste management to how we treat people in our communities. If you are deemed unmanageable or a criminal, it is normal to prescribe medications and chemicals for you and perhaps even send you to the holding cell in either a mental treatment facility or prison. Here, you may tragically be treated like wasted life without intrinsic value.

When I saw the similarities in these two systems, I realized how our civilization addresses these problems in a linear fashion. If we use the waste from the composting toilet it will provide needed fertility to our food forest. This saves us from purchasing fertilizer and benefits the whole system while decreasing the need for waste management at the same time. Similarly, if we utilize the skills and talents of individuals which have been branded as undesirable, it will increase the diversity of our community. By employing resources that would otherwise be wasted, we conserve energy and could provide purpose and meaning to an otherwise discarded reserve. There are no throw away people.

Every season has a purpose. The springtime brings new life into the cycle. Seeds will sprout in this time as the world wakes from its winter sleep. Summertime is filled with growth and is the time to do work. This is where we tend the garden the most and do the majority of the hard work on the land. In the fall we enjoy the harvest. This is a time filled with celebration and appreciation for all the work we have done and for Nature's abundance. In the winter we may slow down and reflect. We can plan for next season and start the whole cycle over again. While we all may have a season we prefer, none can be removed from the cycle and each is vital and precious.

I have seen this natural cycle reflected in the Medicine Wheel, also known as the Sacred Hoop used by the Native Americans. The Medicine Wheel is a tool used in ceremonies, teachings, and therapies by the native people of North America. It embodies the four directions which symbolize dimensions of health and the cycles of life. Each one is valuable and all are an integral part of the wheel. In the system it is easy to see how every season needs to be present in the year, just as all people need to be present in humanity. We must not ignore any season because we do not appreciate the weather, just as we must not ignore any person because we do not like their actions. We can use the wisdom of the Medicine Wheel to help inspire us to see the limitless potential of everyone with whom we will share this sacred space of Mother Earth. As we spend more time cherishing the beauty in this amazing tapestry of life, it may become easier to start appreciating all the relationships involved in creating this beauty.

As we create cultures that value acceptance, it is easier to appreciate that all life has intrinsic value. If we can truly include everyone into our communities and empower them to live their passion, then everyone will have more opportunity to reap the benefits of an abundant and regenerative social system.

Activity 10:
Create a Project in your Community

What would you want your future to look like and what actions will bring you the greatest happiness?

- Using the list of your needs discovered in Activity 3, take time to establish an activity that ties them all together. For example, if your needs included: growing food, teaching others, and helping people, then an appropriate activity would be "Farming" or "Teaching." Identify an activity that truly brings you joy.
- After you have established a preferred activity, identify people in your community who would benefit the most from your service. For example, perhaps there is a homeless population in your area who would greatly benefit from learning how to grow organic food. Identify a group of people that you really want to help.
- Write a step by step plan of action for how you will deliver these services to the group of people you identified. In our example this could include donating food that you have grown to a local food pantry or beginning a free class on how to grow organic food. There is no project too large or too small.
- The only rule for this activity is that you should not make any profit. Any money that is donated to you should be returned back into the project.

This exercise could have the greatest impact on your life by dynamically transforming your passion into action in a way that serves your community. After you have done this activity for three weeks, ask yourself if you want to continue. Perhaps this could be your new full-time job and you can re-design the project to provide your living wage requirements. Start to visualize yourself in this new role serving your community, providing for yourself and your family, while expressing your true passion.

CHAPTER 12

Integration

"In nature we never see anything isolated, but everything is in connection with something else which is before it, beside it, under it, and over it."

- Johann Wolfgang von Goethe

WE HAVE EXPLORED NUMEROUS TOOLS that you may use to design your life into one filled with abundance and happiness. At this point, if you have read each chapter, completed all the activities, and identified at least one life passion, we can now attempt to integrate these tools into your life and practice sharing the new paradigm with the people around you.

Independently, each tool is valuable and will be a wonderful addition to your life, and their effects are compounded when they are implemented together. Like the spokes of the wheel, they strengthen each other and provide greater stability when combined. Integration of the whole makes each individual challenge easier to overcome.

Spend some time practicing the activities at the end of each chapter and organize each under the appropriate chapter heading. For example, if you now do a morning exercise routine you could put that into a list labeled "Wellness and Health." This illustrates how you are currently using your time and will show how balanced and diverse your day is. It is very common to focus on activities you enjoy and have acquired proficiency in because there is satisfaction in the accomplishment that goes with mastering a skill. Imagine you are a yoga student. Committed yoga students will focus on developing their breathing, developing flexibility, and deepening their meditation practice. I have seen many extremely flexible individuals refuse to spend time developing other key aspects of the practice. This results in an isolated proficiency that makes further advancement harder. This is similar to bodybuilders who spend time developing particular muscle groups while ignoring others. It is when attention is given to the system as a whole that the greatest growth can be observed.

After you have sorted each activity, review the list and see which chapter categories are favored and which could use more attention. The more diverse your life becomes; the more resilient you will be in the face of unforeseen challenges.

No one can avoid life's challenging situations, and disturbance is an important part of every ecosystem. Every disturbance has a unique function. Forest fires cycle nutrients and clear undergrowth, allowing for new trees to sprout. When an old tree falls in the forest, it gives room for new trees to grow. A hurricane will spread seeds, break up red tides, and help balance global heat as it moves through an area. These disturbances are beneficial as well as destructive. We can view the challenges in our lives in the same way. Losing a job can cause financial burden for your family but can also provide you with the opportunity to begin a new job that brings you greater happiness.

I believe it is most important to start with yourself when making these important changes. You should be able to provide a living example to your community of a healthy and happy human to demonstrate that this way of life is realistic and obtainable. As you change your life into one filled with love and abundance, others will see this and notice. The best way to provoke change is by being the change you want to see in the world.

I remember the day I recognized this joy in the eyes of a friend. I can't remember any actions or words he said, but I remember the feeling in my heart. I remember thinking "I want to feel that happy." I asked, "What do I need to do to achieve that level of bliss?" No one could have convinced me that I wanted to change my life, but once I felt it in my heart, no one could convince me otherwise.

Can your happiness really affect others? The butterfly effect is a phenomenon where a small localized change in a complex system can have large effects elsewhere. A common example of this is the idea that when a butterfly flaps its wings, it could cause a typhoon on the other side of the planet. I like to use this concept as a framework for understanding how our actions affect the planet.

Many of us will never see phytoplankton, but we often make choices in our lifestyles that impact them. As humanity overfishes the oceans for food, we remove important predators that feed on krill and other plankton. This causes an increase in their population resulting in more phytoplankton being consumed. These microscopic organisms are responsible for removing about a third of the CO2 on the planet, and the very air that we breathe depends on their survival. Our relationship with them is intricately connected. Every relationship on this planet is very precious and can often go unseen and unappreciated. You never know who is watching your kindness or act of courage to use as inspiration in their lives. We are all teachers and we are all leaders.

Humans have been evolving for over six million years. I do not believe that we advanced from single cell creatures, learned to use tools and fire, and developed the ability for complex thought, only to sit in traffic and compare ourselves to Hollywood celebrities. I believe we have a responsibility to utilize this gift of human consciousness for the advancement of all life. It doesn't matter what side of the boat you are on if it is sinking; we will all go down. We are faced with many planetary challenges including climate change, social injustice, and the global spread of a toxic consumer culture. These problems affect every man, woman, and child on the planet. Once you decide that you do not want to add to these problems, you become part of the solution.

As humans, we have a history of creating even more problems with our solutions. For example, aphids are a common problem in most gardens. This challenge can be very simple to overcome with soap and water on the leaves or the introduction of ladybugs and other beneficial insects. Commercial agriculture has taken a different approach. Neonicotinoids were developed in the 1990s in response to the aphid infestations. This nicotine-based insecticide has an adverse reaction on pollinators that come in contact with the poison. We have seen significant decreases in bee populations with the increase of neonicotinoid insecticide use. Scientists believe this has been caused in part by the insecticide affecting the bee's memory and navigation abilities. Upon being exposed to the poison, the bee colonies weaken, making them more susceptible to attack by varroa mites. These mites attack the bees while transmitting a virus into the colony that can deform the insects' wings and eventually can cause the hive to collapse. The beekeepers may then choose to use a chemical named Amitraz to treat the mites. Although human poisoning is rare from Amitraz, human exposure can cause drowsiness, convulsions, respiratory depression, and vomiting. This is a long list of problems that have been introduced in response to aphids, which could have easily been treated with soap and water.

I enjoy coaching people and introducing new methods of relating with nature. I host immersion classes and workshops which help people disconnect from technology and stressful routines so they can be more purpose-driven, happier, and live more abundant lives. In these retreats we deeply explore nature and observe her perfection as evolutionary examples of natural systems in balance. We practice designing our lives to imitate the perfection found in nature. This can be a life-changing experience that opens the heart and dares individuals to see the world with new eyes.

One of the most common challenges people share after attending these workshops is going back to the lives they knew before. It can be very alarming to acknowledge the life you were living was not satisfying and realize that it did not bring you the happiness you anticipated. I have had numerous people attend immersion retreats only to return home, quit their jobs, and start completely new lives. After spending periods of time living unguarded with an open heart, it can be difficult to interact with people who have not had the same experience. It can be painful living in modern society with an open heart, and casual interactions can seem superficial.

The period of integration that follows a heart-opening immersion retreat can be shocking, and you may find many new challenges. I recommend taking your time with this integration period. Try to surround yourself with people you can trust and that you respect. This is a very fertile time in your life, and the people you surround yourself with are vital in determining how your life will evolve. I recommend not spending excess time on superficial relationships that lower your energetic vibration or make you feel bad. Engage in activities that support the goals you want to achieve and slowly start reducing the activities that do not. After some time of living your newly designed life of passion, you may start to observe parts of your old life that are falling away. Let them. I like to think of this state of living as waking into your dream, every day.

I have observed people separate their professional and personal lives creating two or more "compartments." I believe it is critical to be proud of the work you do and for it to be a reflection of your identity. If you are a person who has already integrated the work you do and your personal life, congratulations for realizing the importance of this.

Ideally, there should be a deep satisfaction when you tell your friends about your job. This can be a challenge to find your perfect job, and it may take a long time, but I strongly recommend searching for a personally rewarding job if you are not happy with the one you have. I love working in the garden on my days off. I realize I am doing the exact same activities whether I am on the clock or not. I was not getting paid for working in the garden, and the work I was doing gave me great pleasure. It was a great accomplishment when my work and my personal life had become truly integrated.

"If you love your job, you'll never work a day in your life." I heard this quotation when I was young, but I understand it more deeply now. If your job is feeding your passion, you will be more dedicated to completing your work. You will be the first one to your job and the last one to leave because you deeply love the work you are doing. When the people you work with see this energy in you, it can trigger a chain reaction that results in a more productive and more enjoyable workplace. You may find after you integrate your work and personal life and start passionately appreciating your work, you may not require as much vacation time. You may find yourself more present in the moment, enjoying what you are doing instead of thinking about the future or daydreaming of the past. This integrated awareness of the present moment can help you obtain a flow state in which you become more productive, accomplishing more than you thought possible, becoming more successful in your work, and obtaining your personal goals.

When my life was not so integrated, I had one persona for work and another for my friends. I had another when I was with my parents and still another when I was with my girlfriend. I felt conflicted because these personas did not always agree. The incongruence caused anxiety and discomfort. When we are born, things are much simpler. We spend our first few years simply trying to understand our own bodies. As we grow from infancy, we learn to talk and interact with the people close to us. Then, around three years old, something very curious happens. We learn to lie. It begins very simply, perhaps hiding something we did wrong or trying to get something that we want. As we develop, we learn how to tell more complicated lies, and we will even introduce additional lies to support the lies that we've already told. Ultimately, we get so proficient at lying that we are able to lie to ourselves. We can convince ourselves to do certain things to make other people happy or dress a certain way so that we fit in better with our friends. These lies cause confusion and make it more difficult for us to follow our true passion.

I have been told that one of the greatest gifts on earth can be found in a good night's sleep. The moment you close your eyes to begin the journey into your subconscious, your mind begins to replay thoughts and memories of your life. What is included in these images is determined by your experiences, life choices, and personal beliefs. It is easier for you to understand your feelings if all of your relationships are built on a foundation of authenticity. If you change the way you behave in different situations, it becomes difficult to understand what authenticity means to you. It is normal for your thoughts and beliefs to change over time, but they should not be pliable based on who you are talking to or what situation you find yourself in. When you understand your personal definition of authenticity, you will find that situations will be affected by your beliefs rather than your beliefs being affected by the situations. Challenging circumstances do not build character, they reveal it.

We are all powerful creators who are constantly influencing the world around us. We are each responsible for our actions, our conversations, and the relationships that we have. Once we begin to understand that we are in control of our thoughts and actions, they can become more beautiful and powerful, and our lives may manifest as a true reflection of our authenticity.

When we choose to integrate our thoughts and actions into one authentic self, we may find that the thoughts and actions that do not support our authentic selves will begin to disappear. We may find it is easier to let go of doubt and insecurity that could hold us back from actualizing the immense greatness of which we are capable.

There are many tools for developing personal authenticity. My favorite book on the subject is *The Four Agreements* by Miguel Ruiz. In this book published in 1997, Ruiz explains that a person's actions are based on a set of agreements that he describes in the text. These agreements include being impeccable with your word, not taking things personally, not making assumptions, and always doing your best. I enjoy the simplicity in which the author explains how these agreements can have a direct impact on the amount of happiness you experience in your life. His work is a brilliant place to start if you are looking for strategies to integrate your thoughts and actions and explore more deeply into understanding your authentic self.

When I first started practicing yoga, my motivation was mostly for exercise and flexibility. I wanted a healthy body and I enjoyed the rigor of the Bikram practice. The heat in the room got me sweating. The fast-paced asanas increased my cardiovascular health, muscle strength, and flexibility. However, I didn't pay attention to how the meditation practices of yoga could provide peace of mind. There was a disconnection of the body and my mind. Now I look at these meditations with great appreciation and they have become some of my favorite parts of the practice. Likewise, when I started my journey into Permaculture, I was rooted deeply into the scientific methodology of creating efficient and regenerative systems. I enjoyed creating beautiful designs and solving the problems each one faced. It was like solving crossword puzzles or math problems. I didn't pay attention to how eating organic food and living in a deeply connected community would create great health in my mind and body. There was an underlying disconnection within me. Today I appreciate the health I have found by living connected to my food and my community.

As we integrate our minds and bodies into one clear authentic union, we can become capable of achieving remarkable things. The more integrated we become, the more we find the benefits as the many different parts of our lives working together and creating more abundance.

I truly hope that you were able to gather a fresh perspective from this book that will help you in designing a happy and abundant life. It is important to remember to be gentle and patient with yourself. Try not to get frustrated if you fall into old patterns or do not reach your goal as quickly as you would like. If you notice yourself returning to negative or destructive behaviors from your past, allow yourself to notice your actions and gently remind yourself of how you want your future to materialize. The ten activities at the end of each chapter are always available for you to practice. For example, if I ever feel ungrounded, I will do the "sit spot" activity from Chapter 3 to help me strengthen my relationship with the earth. The activities have been designed to evolve and follow you as you grow.

Thank you for allowing me the privilege of sharing my story and thoughts with you. I believe the most precious thing we have is our time, and I am grateful you have chosen to spend some of yours reading the words I have written. I hope you are able to adopt these techniques into your life and are able to find abundance and happiness all around you. You are a perfect infinite being manifested here on Earth to set your passion into action.

Now, what do you need to do today to live a more authentic life?

May you find all the happiness you deserve.

Made in the USA
Columbia, SC
16 November 2021